write

your

will

Susie Munro

Published in 2009 by Age Concern Books

1268 London Road, London SW16 4ER, United
Kingdom

ISBN: 978 0 86242 442 8

A catalogue record for this book is available from the British Library.

Copyright © Age Concern England 2009

The right of Susie Munro to be identified as the author of this work has been asserted by her in accordance with the Copyright, Designs and Patents Act 1988.

The four national Age Concerns in the UK have joined together with Help the Aged to form new national charities dedicated to improving the lives of older people.

Edited by Jana Elles

Cover design by Vincent McEvoy

Designed and typeset by Design and Media Solutions, Maidstone

Printed and bound in Great Britain by Bell & Bain Ltd, Glasgow

Mixed Sources

Product group from well-managed forests and other controlled sources
www.fsc.org Cert no. TT-COC-002769
© 1996 Forest Stewardship Council

Contents

Introduction

This simple guide explains how to go about making your will, your options for getting advice or what to be aware of if you do decide to write it yourself. It also explains why it's important to make one and what might happen if you don't. This isn't a practical guide for people who are sitting down to write their own will without further advice, so you won't find templates to follow or suggested wording. Because it's important to make sure your will is going to be valid and effective in carrying out your wishes, we recommend getting advice on making it.

It also covers related areas such as how to deal with someone's estate after their death and inheritance tax. The guide also looks at lasting powers of attorney and advance decisions (sometimes known as living wills). These are measures you can take to make sure people know what you would like to happen if you are ever unable to make decisions for yourself.

The nature of the subject matter of this guide means that it tackles issues we would often prefer not to think about – your own death, what would happen if friends or family die before you and what would happen if you are no longer able to make decisions for yourself. The guide tries to show how planning for these things can make it easier for others during difficult times and can give you some peace of mind knowing that your wishes should be carried out.

The book refers to the position in England and Wales. Differences in Scotland and Northern Ireland are pointed out in some areas but you should seek further information if you live, or own property, outside of England and Wales. Chapter 9 includes suggestions for getting further information on the position in Scotland and Northern Ireland.

Why make a will?

According to a survey by the National Consumer Council almost two thirds of people in England and Wales do not have a will. The most common reason given for not making a will was that people simply 'hadn't got around to it'.

Other common reasons were that they had never thought about it, they thought they were too young to make a will, they didn't like to think about dying or that they thought their **estate** was not large enough for them to need a will. Only 4% of people said that they were confident that their estate would go to who they wanted, whether or not they had a will.

There are two main reasons for making a will: to make sure that your wishes are carried out and to make things easier for the people who are left behind after your death. This chapter looks at the consequences of not making a will and why, if you're one of the people still putting it off, it might be time to take things into your own hands.

What is a will?

By making a will you are setting out a statement of your wishes, intending it to be legally binding after your death. The main purpose of a will is to say how you want your money, belongings and property to be distributed after your death. It can also be used for other things, such as what you would like your funeral to be like, but there may be more appropriate ways of letting people know these kinds of things.

It's also worth noting that a will is only valid if it meets certain requirements, such as being signed and witnessed properly (these requirements are looked at in chapter 4). If there is any doubt over whether you fully understood what you were doing when you made it, or whether you had been put under pressure to make it by someone else, it could be challenged.

Do you need to make a will?

You might have thought about making a will but decided that you don't need to, or that it's not worth it. The following are some of the common reasons people give for not making a will:

'I don't have enough money to need a will'

This may be true if you are happy for everything to go to the person who would be entitled under the **intestacy rules** (the rules that set out who inherits your money and possessions if you don't leave a will - see page 5), but this won't necessarily be the case. Making a will allows you to make individual gifts, which can mean a lot to people, no matter how small in value. It also allows you to choose the best person to sort things out after you die (your **executor**).

The amounts spouses and civil partners inherit under the intestacy rules have recently been increased but they still may not fully reflect the rise in house prices over the years. So if you own your own home, even if the rest of your estate is of relatively low value, you might be surprised at what would happen if you don't make a will. If you have a spouse or civil partner, you might have assumed that everything would go to them but the examples below show that this may not be the case and, in some situations it may be necessary to sell the house in order to distribute your belongings correctly.

'It's too expensive'

It may cost less than you think, or nothing at all. In chapter 3 we look at some of the different ways of making a will. You may be entitled to the services of a solicitor through a union, or you may qualify for Legal Aid. There are schemes for getting your will writer for free, or in exchange for a donation to charity. Although making a will can sometimes seem expensive, the cost of sorting things out after you die if you don't have a valid will could be much higher.

'I've only got debts and they die with me so it's not an issue'

This isn't the case – as many of your debts as possible will have to be paid out of what you do have, and this must be done in a particular order of priority. Someone will have to be responsible for sorting this out and, if you don't make a will, this job might fall to someone you wouldn't have chosen.

'Making a will is so complicated I'd only make it worse'

In some cases a will can be relatively straightforward, although it is very important to ensure that a will is valid and that it truly reflects what you want to happen. That's why it's usually best to get advice from an expert. You may be surprised how straightforward it could be with help from someone who knows what they're doing. There are options for getting professional help that may cost less than you think. Your will can be changed or scrapped if you change your mind about anything and it remains confidential up until you die.

'My family get on so well they won't need a bit of paper to tell them how to sort it out fairly'

Even if there aren't going to be disputes, a will could help your family be sure about your wishes and make them happier that they're doing what you wanted. It will be a difficult time for them and you might want to take away the responsibility and potential stress involved in trying to work out what the right thing is to do.

'I don't like to think about dying'

This probably applies to most of us but, as you've started reading this book, you're probably not in complete denial that this will eventually happen. Be assured that making your will won't speed up the arrival of the time when it will be needed.

What happens if you die without making a will?

If you die without making a will, or your will turns out to be invalid, you are said to have died **intestate**. This means that your estate – that is, everything you own including money, possessions, **investments** and property after any bills, debts or costs (e.g. funeral costs) are paid – will be distributed according to the intestacy rules. The law dictates who will inherit your estate and, to some extent, how much they will inherit. It also sets out who will be responsible for dealing with your estate. These rules are based on relationships defined by family structures that increasingly do not reflect how people live today. For example, the intestacy rules do not provide for unmarried couples or stepchildren.

The important thing to note here is that your wishes, or those of your family and friends, will have no bearing on how your estate is distributed. When determining who should inherit or manage your estate under the intestacy rules it is irrelevant how close you were to someone, how much contact you had with them or how trustworthy they are. There is no consideration of the comparative needs of family and friends or of reasons, sentimental or economic, why it might be appropriate for certain people to inherit certain things. There is also no opportunity for your money to go to charities or organisations that mean a lot to you, unless you provide for this in your will.

Who inherits your things under the intestacy rules if you die without a will?

The intestacy rules described below only apply in England and Wales. For information on where you can find out about the situation in Scotland and Northern Ireland see chapter 9.

If you are married, or have a civil partner, and you have children

Your spouse or civil partner will get the first £250,000 worth of your estate, all your personal possessions and a **life interest** (see below) in half of what remains. Your children will then get the other half of what remains, divided among them equally. This means that if you have less than £250,000 then your children get nothing, unless your spouse or civil partner gives it to them. (This is the case even if you are separated but not divorced.)

For the purposes of the intestacy rules, your personal possessions are treated separately from the rest of your estate. Your personal possessions means all your belongings except your money, any investments, your house or any other property. So it includes any vehicles, furniture and jewellery.

A life interest means that the person is entitled to benefit from the money or assets during their lifetime, but they cannot dispose of it before their own death. So if the money is invested, your spouse or partner has the right to the interest from it during their lifetime but they cannot spend the capital. On their death, the capital then passes to the children. If the estate includes the family home, the spouse or civil partner is entitled to live in it during their lifetime.

> **Jaspreet dies leaving a wife, Harvinder, and two children Balbir and Daljit**. His estate is worth £350,000.
> £250,000 goes to Harvinder and she also gets a life interest in half of the **remainder**, i.e. £50,000. If this is invested, she is entitled to the interest, but she cannot spend any of the £50,000 itself. Balbir and Daljit get a half share of the remaining £50,000, i.e. £25,000 each. On Harvinder's death, the £50,000 passes to the children, so they get another £25,000 each (plus anything else they inherit from her).

Children

Under the intestacy rules, if your estate is to go to your children this includes legally adopted children and your children from previous relationships, but not stepchildren. If you have stepchildren who you want to benefit from your estate you need to make a will. It's not relevant that your children have grown up; 'children' refers to adult children as well. If you had a child who has died before you leaving children of their own, anything your child would have been entitled to will pass to the next generation, your grandchildren.

If you are married, or have a civil partner, but have no children

Your spouse or civil partner will get the first £450,000, all of your personal possessions and half of what remains. The other half of this remainder goes to your parents or, if your parents have died before you, your brothers and sisters or their children. If you have no living parents, brothers, sisters, nieces or nephews, then your spouse or civil partner inherits everything. Half-brothers and half-sisters do not count in this situation, they would not inherit anything.

Paul and Connor are civil partners. They have no children. When Paul dies his estate is worth £500,000 (after payment of **inheritance tax,** see chapter 6). Most of this is the value of the house he owned, where he lived with Connor. Paul's parents both died before him, as did his sister Jean. His brother John and Jean's daughter Beth are still alive.

Connor will get £450,000 plus £25,000. The remaining £25,000 is shared equally between John and Beth. As most of Paul's estate is made up of the house he owned and lived in with Connor, it's possible that Connor would have to sell the house in order to pay the £25,000 to John and Beth.

If you are not married, or in a civil partnership, and you have children

The whole of your estate will be divided between your children equally. If any of them have died before you, leaving children of their own, then your grandchildren will inherit their parent's share.

> **James had two children, Philip and Rachel.** James is not married or in a civil partnership. Philip died before James, leaving three children of his own. On James' death his estate is worth £12,000.
> Had Philip been alive when James died, Philip and Rachel would have shared the estate equally, each inheriting £6,000. As Philip has died, his share is divided equally between his own children. So Rachel inherits £6,000 and each of Philip's three children inherits a third each of their father's share, i.e. £2,000 each.

If you are not married, or in a civil partnership, and have no children

Your whole estate will pass to your nearest relatives, which is worked out in the following order:

1. Parents
2. Brothers and sisters, or if they die before you, their children or grandchildren
3. Half-brothers and half-sisters
4. Grandparents
5. Uncles and aunts or, if they die before you, their children or grandchildren (this does not include uncles and aunts related to you by marriage only)
6. Your parents' half-brothers and half-sisters (i.e. who only share one parent)

7. If there is no one in any of the above categories your estate will go to the Crown.

So if both of your parents are still alive, they will share the estate. If only one of them is still alive they will inherit the whole estate. If they have both died before you, everything will be shared equally by any brothers or sisters, or their offspring and so on.

> **Ellen had lived with her partner Leon for twenty five years before she died.** They were not married and had no children. Ellen's parents both died before her and she had no brothers or sisters. Her father had a brother who died leaving one son, Ellen's cousin Robert, who she had not seen for over thirty years. The whole of Ellen's estate, no matter how much it is worth, will go to Robert. Leon will not be entitled to anything.

The intestacy rules are strict and sometimes a big asset, such as a house, has to be sold so the whole estate can be divided up according to the rules – even if someone is still living there as their home. It may be possible for friends and family to reach an agreement to avoid this but the easiest way to avoid a dispute is to make a will.

What can people do if they aren't entitled to anything under the intestacy rules?

Someone who was dependent on you financially who is not provided for under the intestacy rules (such as an unmarried partner, stepchild or a friend or carer who lived with you) can make a claim through the court for part of your estate. If no agreement can be reached, it would be for the court to decide whether they should receive anything. You can never be sure that there will be no disagreement between your friends and family over your estate but making your wishes clear in your will can reduce the risk of conflict and the cost, not to mention the distress, involved in going to court.

If you have no relatives and your estate goes to the Crown, the Treasury Solicitor can make *ex gratia* (this means they are under no obligation to do so) payments out of the estate. This could be to a charity that you had close links with or to a friend or unmarried partner, for example. Whether such a payment is made is entirely at the discretion of the Crown.

To apply for an ex gratia payment, the person has to contact the Bona Vacantia department of the Treasury Solicitor and explain why they think they are entitled to something from the estate. See chapter 9 for contact details.

Who deals with your estate if you don't leave a will?

If you die without leaving a valid will, there are rules setting out who deals with your estate (see chapter 8); paying your debts and distributing everything to the people who are entitled. This will usually be your nearest relative, who may or may not be the most appropriate person to take on the role or they may not want to do it. It could be better to use a will to choose the person you think is most suitable.

Summary

The law does provide solutions for deciding what happens if you die without having made a will but it is unlikely that the rules of intestacy would result in your estate going to the people you would have chosen in exactly the way you would have chosen. It is also unlikely that it would result in the best outcomes for the people left to deal with the estate and for those who might expect to inherit something from you.

Making a will allows you to take control over what happens after your death and even though you won't be around to see the results, the people who benefit from your forward planning will almost certainly appreciate it.

2
What should be in your will?

Before you write your will, whether or not you decide to take professional legal advice, there are some important things you need to consider. By thinking about what money and possessions you have to leave in your will (the estate), who you want your estate to go to (the **beneficiaries**) and who you want to deal with your estate after your death (the executors) you'll have a much better idea about what other things you need further advice or information on. This chapter explores some of the questions you need to ask yourself and the decisions you will have to make.

What will be included in your estate?

You need to think about what is likely to make up your estate. This will include everything you own at your death. Before seeing a solicitor or **will writer**, or writing your own will, you should try to make a list of everything that would make up your estate, including property, cash, possessions, investments, shares, shares in your own company, vehicles etc. You also need to take into account any debts or money that may be owing at your death, such as funeral costs or outstanding bills, as these will have to be paid before the estate can be distributed.

If you are leaving a house or other property which may still have a mortgage outstanding, you should consider whether the mortgage is to be paid off out of the estate before the gift is made or whether the **beneficiary** is to take over the mortgage. Unless you specify otherwise, a mortgage will be dealt with like other debts and paid off out of the estate. However, this could require the sale of the house to raise funds to pay off the mortgage.

If you rent your home your tenancy does not form part of your estate so you can't leave it in your will. If you live with other people, their right to stay on after you die will depend on the type of tenancy agreement you have and their relationship to you. You should seek advice from an advice agency if this is relevant to you.

Of course it will be impossible to predict the exact size or value of your estate on your death. You will have sold or lost some items and gained others and the value of any investments will hopefully have gone up but could also have gone down. There are ways of drafting your will to account for this; these are looked at later in this chapter.

Jointly owned property

When thinking about how to distribute your estate, it's important to take into account any joint property. If you jointly own property, such as a house or land, with someone else, it will either be held as **joint tenants** or **tenants in common** (these are the legal terms for the types of ownership – it is nothing to do with renting property). This will depend on what you agreed when you made the purchase (unless you changed the agreement at a later date). If you want to check what kind of ownership you have, you could check with the Land Registry or, if you still have the paperwork from when you bought the property, this should have been confirmed in writing at the time. Usually, property owned together by a couple is held as joint tenants, but you should check before making your will, as it will have a big impact on the value of your estate.

Joint tenancy

If a property is held as joint tenants, on the death of one tenant their share automatically passes to the other tenant. So, for example, if you own a flat with your partner as joint tenants, on your death your share will automatically pass to your partner, who will then own the whole flat themselves. You cannot leave your share to someone else in your will as the joint tenancy is an agreement between you and your co-owner which cannot be overridden by your will.

Tenants in common

If you own a property as tenants in common, your share can be passed on to someone else on your death. The other co-owner(s) would retain their share but would become joint owners with whoever you left your share to in your will.

Note that in Scotland all joint property is held as tenants in common, unless you have expressly agreed in the ownership documents that it should pass to the survivor on the death of the first partner.

Money in a joint bank account automatically passes to the other joint account holder, so you can't leave it to someone else in your will.

Who do you want to leave things to in your will?

A major decision to make is who you want to inherit from your estate. This may seem straightforward but there are some important considerations to bear in mind and it may be the bit that requires most thinking about. Before you begin to write your will you should have a clear plan of which individuals, organisations or charities you would like to benefit. Anyone you leave anything to in your will, i.e. who 'benefits' from your will, is known as a beneficiary.

Below are some things to be aware of when deciding who will be your beneficiaries. Once you have decided who you wish to benefit, you may need to take advice about how you can best put your wishes into effect.

Leaving something to a child under 18

You can leave something to a child but they cannot inherit legal ownership of it until they are 18 (or 16 in Scotland). The gift would be held in **trust** until they are old enough to inherit (trusts are explained later in this chapter). This means that while they can enjoy the use of whatever you have left them, they do not legally own it and so cannot sell it or give it away, for example. You could use your will to specify a higher age if 18 seems too young for them to be able to take on responsibility for their inheritance.

If you are responsible for bringing up any children under 18, you can use your will to appoint someone to be their guardian should you die whilst they are still under 18. You shouldn't assume that your spouse or someone else with parental responsibility would necessarily be able to continue to care for the children after your death, as, for example, they might die before or at the same time as you.

Leaving something to someone who does not have mental capacity to look after it themselves

You may have a beneficiary in mind who may need help to manage the gift that you leave them, for example if you want to leave some money or property to someone who has dementia or learning difficulties. There may already be arrangements in place for someone else (an **attorney** or **deputy**) to make decisions about their finances and property (this is explained in chapter 5). If not, this could be another situation where a trust might be appropriate.

Leaving something to someone who is on benefits

If you leave money or property to someone who is in receipt of state benefits it could have an effect on their entitlement. If they are on a type of benefit which is affected by how much money they have (i.e. a 'means-tested' benefit), your gift could affect how much they get or stop their benefit altogether, until some of the money has been spent. Don't be put off including them, but to make sure they benefit as much as possible from your gift, it can be worth getting advice. A local advice centre such as Age Concern or a Citizens Advice Bureau should be able to advise on benefits. Again, you could consider setting up a trust if this is going to be an issue.

Leaving something to a charity

You could also consider leaving money, or another kind of gift, to a charity. You need to be clear exactly which charity you intend to benefit, so make sure the full correct name, address and charity number are included. Many large charities will be able to advise you on how to do this or you could take advice from a solicitor.

You can also appoint a charity to be your executor, which may be appropriate if you intend to leave all or most of your estate to the charity. You should discuss this with the charity first of all and get advice on how to do it.

Charities receive a large proportion of their income from **legacies** and many depend on them to be able to continue their work. The number of charities to choose from is huge and could seem overwhelming. You may already have a charity in mind that you have links with, perhaps because someone close to you has benefited directly from their work. Or you might have a particular type of work in mind such as medical research, working with young people or older people, an arts organisation or one working in human rights.

The Charities Aid Foundation provides a search facility on its website where you can search for local, national or international charities according to the type of work they do. You might find one that you've not heard of before that you would like to support. It can also advise on leaving a legacy to a charity. It can also act as a trustee of the gift you leave for a particular charity and can take care of the formalities of setting up a trust.

Different types of gift you can make in your will

There are a number of ways in which you can leave your estate to your beneficiaries. When you leave something in your will, your gift is called a legacy or a **bequest**. The two terms are interchangeable. If you go for professional advice on making your will, or you are following guidance on writing your own, it may help to understand the terms used for different types of gift. Below are some of the different ways of leaving things to people.

Leaving a specific item or amount

If you leave someone a particular named item such as your house, your car or a particular piece of furniture then this would be called a **specific legacy**. If it is a specific amount of money it would be known as a **pecuniary legacy**.

It is important to make sure there is no uncertainty over what it was you intended to leave and who exactly you wished to benefit. For example, if you say you intend to leave your car to your friend James, there could be confusion if at the time of your death you have two cars or you've sold your car and bought a van or if more than one person called James considers that they were a friend of yours. Be as specific as you can, including as many details about the gift as you can and the full names and addresses of your beneficiaries and a description of their relationship to you. You don't have to update your will each time one of your beneficiaries moves but including addresses at the time you write it can help to be clear exactly who it is you are thinking of.

Leaving the remainder of your estate

It is important to make sure that the whole of your estate is dealt with, with nothing left unaccounted for. The way to do this is to name someone who will inherit the remainder of your estate – i.e. everything that remains after all the specific gifts have been made. This type of gift is called a **residuary legacy**. You can state that the remainder is to be shared between a number of people or charities and set out the proportions in which it is to be divided.

There will almost always be a remainder, as it will be impossible at the time of drafting your will for you to predict exactly what you will have when you die. If you don't leave a residuary legacy, it is very likely that there will be parts of your estate left over which are not covered by your will; this is called a **partial intestacy**. The rules of intestacy will be applied to determine who inherits the remainder (see chapter 1). This will also happen if you do name someone to inherit the remainder but they die before you.

Leaving items or money in trust for someone

By setting up a trust, you appoint people as trustees to hold property or money for the benefit of someone else. This is particularly useful if the person you want to leave money or property to would not be able to manage it without help, for example, because they have dementia or they are a child. So, for example, you could appoint your daughter to be trustee of money you want to leave for your grandson until he turns 21. He could benefit from it before his 21st birthday, for example, by your daughter buying certain things for his benefit and then at 21 he would inherit it to deal with himself.

You can use your will to set up a trust. You can set out rules for the trustees to follow and there are different types of trust which allow a greater amount of discretion for the trustees to decide how to use the assets. A trust can be very straightforward, and need not be costly to set up and administrate, but you should take legal advice on how to set it up, the most appropriate type of trust and implications such as whether it will affect how much tax is paid on your estate.

Leaving someone a life interest in something

Another type of legacy is a **life interest** in something. It can be used for property or some other part of your estate. The person with the life interest benefits from the gift during their lifetime, without having full legal ownership, and then on their death ownership passes to someone else. For example, you could leave a sum of money to your partner to benefit from the income during their lifetime (for example from the interest or dividends if it is invested) and specify that the capital is to pass to your children on the death of your partner. This means that your partner can't spend the money during their lifetime and you can be sure the capital will eventually pass to your children.

Similarly, if you ultimately want to leave your house to your children, but a friend or carer (who is not a joint owner) lives with you, you may not want them to be made homeless if you die and leave your house to your children. You can give them a life interest in the house giving the right to live in it for as long as they want.

Making provision for possible future changes

One way to ensure that your will is still effective if things change in the future is to make a **contingent legacy**. This is a way of saying what you want to happen if something has changed. For example, you can name someone to inherit in the event that someone else you have left things to dies before you do. You can also name more than one person, or charity, to share the remainder. Taking these steps can avoid a partial intestacy.

You can make provision in your will for what would happen if your estate is not large enough on your death to meet all your intended gifts by listing an order of priority in which the gifts are to be made until there is insufficient for the last ones to be made.

Who do you want to choose as your executors?

If you leave a will, someone has to be responsible for reading it and making sure that your wishes are carried out. In your will you should say who you want to do this. The people you choose to deal with your estate after your death – collecting in all your assets, paying debts and tax and distributing the estate to the beneficiaries – are called executors. You need to choose someone (or more than one person) who you trust to carry out your wishes and who will be able to cope with the practicalities and responsibility of the role. This could be a friend or relative, or a professional such as a solicitor. It does not matter if they are a beneficiary of your will or not.

A maximum of four executors can act under your will. You can name only one executor but this places a lot of responsibility on one person and could be a problem if they are unable or unwilling to act when the tlme comes. This risk can be reduced by naming more than one executor or by naming a replacement to be appointed if your preferred executor dies before you or cannot act for any reason.

Naming more than one executor can mean that they are able to support each other and share the responsibility. However, they will all have equal rights to deal with the estate so there could be difficulties if you choose people who don't get on or who may find it difficult to reach agreement on how best to carry out your wishes.

Choosing family or friends as executors

If you are choosing a friend or family member as executor you should try to choose someone who is organised and good at dealing with paperwork, particularly if they are going to have to arrange the payment of inheritance tax on your estate (see chapter 6). Above all you must be sure that you can trust their integrity and be confident that they will carry out your wishes as set out in the will.

People often choose their partner, or another close family member, to be the executor. This has the benefit that they are likely to know about what possessions and property will make up your estate, where you keep things and how to contact beneficiaries and others involved. They are also likely to be the main beneficiary, which makes distribution of the estate easier. But they are also likely to be the people who are most upset and at their least able to cope at the time they are faced with the practicalities of dealing with your estate.

Being an executor can mean a lot of work and responsibility. If they make a mistake, they can face claims on the estate from people who think they should have inherited something. There is also the possibility that, if they don't pay off all debts before distributing the estate, they could be personally liable to pay anything left owing. It is not something to be taken lightly, so you should discuss it with the people you have in mind before naming them in your will. You must be sure they are actually prepared to take on the role.

If you don't have family or friends who would be appropriate executors, you could appoint a professional executor, such as a solicitor (see below). Or if you intend to leave a large amount of your estate to a charity, you could consider appointing the charity as executor. You should contact them to discuss this with them first.

Choosing a professional as your executor

You may decide it's best to have someone who is not close to you to be your executor. This would probably depend on the nature and value of your estate: for example, if you have complicated investments, property overseas or your own business, you might need to appoint a professional or at least a friend or family member with the required expertise and experience.

People who choose to appoint professional executors will usually choose a solicitor, accountant or bank. These people will charge for their services and this will come out of the estate. If you do appoint a professional it's important you check how much they will charge as this will affect how much you expect to be able to pass on to your beneficiaries. The costs can be substantial. Solicitors will generally charge between 1%-3% of the value of the estate, or will charge for the work they do based on an hourly rate, and banks usually charge more than solicitors. The fee could increase with the number of beneficiaries, as an estate that has to be distributed to many different people will involve more work.

If you choose a professional executor, it is very difficult for the beneficiaries to challenge the amount they charge to carry out your will, or to remove the executor if they are not happy with the work they are doing, so make sure you are happy with the services and terms on offer before making a final decision.

If you name a specific solicitor rather than a firm, they may have retired or moved job by the time you die, so be sure that you are clear about what you'd want to happen in this case.

If you don't appoint a professional, the people you do choose can seek expert advice if they need it and this would be paid for out of the estate. If you appoint family or friends as executors, they can claim their expenses out of the estate but cannot charge for the time that they spend carrying out the role.

What else do you want your will to cover?

As well as distributing your property, a will is sometimes used to express any other wishes you have about what happens after you die, although these instructions are not legally binding. You could use it, for example, to explain what you would like to happen at your funeral or what you'd like to happen to your pets. It's best to discuss these requests with the people involved before including them in your will, to make sure they are happy to take on the responsibility and that what you are suggesting is practical.

Your funeral

As mentioned above, you can use your will to state your preferences for your funeral. For example, you may want to say whether you want to be buried or cremated. You might want to state that, rather than the traditional flowers, you would like people to donate money to a particular charity or that you don't want people to wear black to the funeral. You can also let people know whether there is any particular music you would like to be played at the ceremony or any poems or readings and who you would like to read them. This can make it easier on the friends or family who are arranging your funeral and who may otherwise be uncertain that they are doing what you would have wanted.

If you don't want to make this too formal, you could put your wishes for your funeral in a separate document instead, for example a letter to your family or executors. That way, if you change your mind about anything, it would be easier to amend.

Funeral Plans

A funeral plan is a way of paying for and arranging your own funeral in advance.

You can either pay a one off fee or pay in instalments. The price is then fixed so that the cost of the funeral is covered even if the real cost has risen significantly by the time it takes place. You should check carefully what is covered by the plan and whether anything extra may be payable at the time of the funeral.

A funeral plan could relieve the burden from friends or family of making the arrangements for your funeral, and finding the money to pay for it if they can't immediately access money from your estate.

Summary

Deciding to make your will is an important first step but there is a lot more to think about before you go ahead and make it. It will help to write a list of what you expect to make up your estate, the people or organisations you would like to benefit, the types of legacies you would like to leave and who you want to be your executors. If you have thought these things through before you get further advice on your will, it should make the process much smoother.

You can buy a funeral plan through Age Concern, but there are many other providers and you should shop around before making a decision. For information about the Age Concern funeral plan you can call 0800 022 32 42.

3

Making a will

There are a few options for how to make a will.
When deciding how to go about it, you need to
consider not just which method you can afford
but also which will be most appropriate for you.
The sorts of things that might influence your
decision may be how complicated your will might
be (for example, do you own property abroad or
do you want to set up a trust?), how confident
you are that you understand how to make a valid
will, and how much your estate is likely to be
worth.

Writing it yourself

For some people a simple letter explaining what
you want to happen to your belongings when you
die may seem like an appealing option. If,
however, your wishes are not drawn up as a valid
will, the people you wanted to leave gifts to will
have no legal right to those things. Only the
people who are entitled to inherit under the
intestacy rules would have the right to your
estate. See chapter 4 for details of what makes a
valid will.

It is possible to write your own will but this is only
recommended in the simplest of circumstances
and only if you are sure you know what you're
doing. It is tempting to think that writing a will

yourself is easy and that it could save you unnecessary expense. However, it's often not that simple. There are a number of hidden pitfalls and problems that you may not have thought of and you could end up either with a will that is not valid or with something that does not express your wishes in the way you wanted.

If a mistake or omission in your will leads to a dispute, the cost of putting things right will almost certainly be greater than what you thought you had saved by doing it yourself. If the mistake is only discovered after your death, it won't be you who has to worry about it, so making things easier for those you leave behind is one of the main reasons for making sure you have a valid will.

If you do decide to write it yourself you need to make sure you understand the legal requirements for a valid will and also that you draft your will in a way which puts your wishes into writing without creating any practical difficulties. You can buy a will pack from a stationer or bookshop; the best of these will have detailed guidance on how to complete your will.

Of course, solicitors and other professionals are not infallible – they can and do sometimes make mistakes. But if they make a mistake, they should have professional indemnity insurance to cover the cost of compensating anyone who loses out as a result. All solicitors are required to have professional indemnity insurance in place; other will writers may have it but you should always check before you use their services. If a will writer does not have professional indemnity insurance, look for someone who does.

Some common problems that can occur with a poorly written will:

- The will doesn't deal with the possibility that a beneficiary could die before you.

- The will doesn't cover all of your estate.

- Gifts are described ambiguously so it's not clear what you intended to leave someone.

- An asset is sold before your death, leaving the intended beneficiary with no inheritance.

- The will is witnessed by someone who is a beneficiary.

- The witnesses weren't present at the time you sign the will, which makes it invalid.

Asking a professional to write your will

Everyone's situation is different, so without advice on your individual circumstances, you may miss something important. Getting professional advice when arranging your will doesn't have to be expensive and is strongly recommended. The main options are to see a solicitor, go to a will-writing company or use a bank or building society.

Using a solicitor

Some solicitors will arrange to visit you at home or will give you an appointment at their offices. If you are put in touch with a solicitor through an organisation such as your union or a motoring organisation, this could be a telephone or online service provided by a national firm. This may be cheaper but you may prefer a local, face-to-face interview.

It's important that you are happy, not only with the amount your solicitor is going to charge, but with the overall service. You might want to ask who will be carrying out the work on your will. It could be a trainee or someone else who is not a solicitor. If so, they should be supervised by a qualified solicitor. It's important that you understand the advice you are given and the work they are planning to do for you and that you are confident that they fully understand your wishes. If you don't understand something, ask them to explain it. If you still don't understand, consider going somewhere else.

If you use a solicitor to draft your will and are not happy with the service or with the way the firm handles your complaint, you can refer your complaint to the Legal Complaints Service (LCS). The LCS has the power to order your solicitor to put the problem right or to pay you compensation. The LCS can sometimes get involved if you are the main beneficiary and have a complaint about how a solicitor executor is handling the estate. You can contact them by phoning 0845 608 6565.

Be wary of will-writing services, including those provided by solicitors, where everything is done online or by post. These involve you completing a standard questionnaire which should give enough information for your will to be written up.

*However, this kind of service can lead to
a complication or misunderstanding
being overlooked, which could have been
identified through face-to-face or
telephone advice.*

How to find a solicitor

Not all solicitors are the same. These days
most specialise in a particular area of law.
Many solicitors will never have drafted a will
so, although it seems obvious, you need to
choose one with the relevant expertise and
experience.

Solicitors who are members of the Society
of Trust and Estate Practitioners are
specialists in this area of law. You can find a
member at www.step.org/findapractitioner.
You can also find a local solicitor through
the Law Society either by calling *Tel: 0870
606 2555* or by searching at
www.lawsociety.org.uk.

Using a will-writing company

There are increasing numbers of businesses
offering will-writing services, provided by people
who do not have legal qualifications. Anyone can
set themselves up as a will writer and charge
people for their services without having any
training, qualifications, insurance or experience.
You should be wary of non-solicitors offering this
service, but that doesn't mean you should
automatically avoid them.

This option is often cheaper than using a
solicitor, and they may be more flexible about

when and where they can offer you an interview, but the absence of compulsory regulation means there is no guarantee of quality and there could be a lack of protection should things go wrong. Many will writers are members of either the Society of Will Writers or the Institute of Professional Will Writers. These are both voluntary regulatory bodies that can offer consumers a degree of confidence in the qualifications, skills and experience of their members. Both bodies have a Code of Practice that their members must follow and both require members to have professional indemnity insurance. You can check with them to find out if someone is a member (see chapter 9).

There is no obligation on will writers to become a member and submit to the regulation of either body. If you are thinking about using a will writer who is not a member of either the Society of Will Writers or the Institute of Professional Will Writers, you should consider whether you can be confident that they have the necessary skills to do a good job and whether procedures are in place to avoid, or deal with, any problems arising in the future as a result of their work.

The lack of regulation of will-writing companies means that there may be a higher risk of problems occurring. Problems that have been reported in the past include excessive fees being charged for storing a will, wills not being stored securely and companies moving premises without notifying customers who had wills stored with them. If the company goes out of business, it may be difficult to trace your will when it is needed.

Using a bank or building society

Many banks and building societies offer will-writing services. These are usually only available if you are appointing the bank as your executor and signing up for other financial services. You should be sure this is what you need and consider all the other options before agreeing to this. If you use a bank or building society, you will have access to the Financial Ombudsman Service if you have a complaint about the service. This is an independent public body which aims to settle disputes between consumers and financial service providers.

If you have professional advice when writing your will, such as from a solicitor or a bank, they may suggest that you appoint them as executor. Before you agree, check what they will charge and consider whether it is necessary to appoint a professional executor at all (see chapter 2).
*Similarly, if whoever writes your will tries to insist on you taking other services from them, such as drawing up a **lasting power of attorney** (see chapter 5) or storing the will for a charge, do not feel obliged to take up these services and think about going elsewhere to have your will written.*

What might it cost to make a will?
Writing your own will

If you do decide you want to do it yourself, you can buy a will pack for around £15. These include guidance and templates for you to use. You don't need to buy a will pack but you would have to be absolutely sure you know what you're doing if you plan to write your own will from scratch.

Using a professional service

The cost of using a professional to draft your will can vary hugely, depending on the nature and complexity of your will and the experience and expertise of the person doing the work. If you do it all online or over the phone it should be cheaper than a face-to-face interview and a non-legally qualified will writer should charge less than a solicitor. As a very rough guide, you could expect to pay around £100 for a basic will drawn up by a will writer and more than this if you see a solicitor.

The best advice is to shop around and compare prices but keep in mind that the cheapest option isn't necessarily the best.

Mirror wills

Some couples create what are called 'mirror wills' where the terms of the wills are almost identical, for example most of the estate is left to the other partner.

If you create a mirror will with your partner, it's important that you make provision for what will happen if you both die at the same time, for example by appointing replacement executors and beneficiaries.

Creating mirror wills usually costs less than if you and your partner create your wills separately. But before you do this, you should be sure that you both want to distribute your estates in the same way.

Help with the cost of writing your will

There are many options for getting professional help with will-writing and you might find that it's cheaper than you expected.

- Check if you might already be entitled to the services of a solicitor through membership of an organisation such as a trade union.

- Free Wills Month is a scheme to encourage people to make a will and to raise money for a number of charities. Through this scheme, if you are over 55 years old you can have a will drawn up for free by a local solicitor. Although there is no obligation to do so, the charities that fund the scheme hope that users of the scheme will leave a gift to them in their will. Free Wills Month runs in different cities and towns at different times of the year. You can visit *www.freewillsmonth.org.uk* to register your interest or call *0845 020 4309*.

- Will Aid is a different scheme operating during November. Participating solicitors will draw up your will in return for a suggested donation to a group of charities. See *www.willaid.org.uk* or call *0300 0300 013* to find a local participating solicitor.

- Legal Aid is available to cover the cost of having a solicitor draw up your will in limited circumstances. To qualify for legal aid to write a will you must have income and capital under certain limits and you must be:

  - aged 70 or over, or
  - disabled, or

- a parent who wishes to provide for their disabled child in their will.

You can find out if you meet the financial requirements by asking a solicitor or by calling the Community Legal Advice helpline *0845 345 4345*. There is also an online legal aid eligibility calculator on the website *www.communitylegaladvice.org.uk*.

Not all solicitors can carry out work under legal aid funding. To find a solicitor who can write your will under legal aid, contact Community Legal Advice.

Summary

How you go about making your will is your choice and may depend on how much you want to spend and the complexity of your plans. Whatever you decide, you should make sure you understand exactly what you're paying for and beware of extra charges for add-on services that you don't want or that should be included in the service anyway. Above all you should have confidence that the will you end up with properly reflects your wishes.

4

Making sure your will is valid

What makes a will valid?

A will does not have to be on any particular form, it can be handwritten and you don't have to use legal language. However, it must be unambiguous as to what your intentions are and there are a few key requirements for it to be valid:

- Your will must be in writing.
- It must be signed by you in the presence of two witnesses.
- The witnesses must also sign it in your presence.
- You must be over age 18 when you make it.
- You must have the mental capacity to understand what you are doing and the effects it will have.
- It must be a genuine reflection of your wishes, not made as a result of pressure from anyone else.

Signing your will

You must sign the will (or direct someone else to sign on your behalf if you are not physically able to) in front of two witnesses, who must then sign the will themselves. Both witnesses must be present when you sign the will and must also be present when the other signs.

If you are blind or partially sighted, or if you have difficulty reading for whatever reason, you can have someone read out the contents of your will to you. You can then sign it yourself, in which case the part of the will you sign must state that the will has been read out to you and you understand and agree it.

Alternatively, if you are not able to sign it yourself, for example if you can't hold a pen, you can direct someone else to sign it on your behalf after it has been read out to you. Again the will must state that this is what has happened and that you fully understand and approve the contents of the will.

The rules about signing your will are different in Scotland. You should take advice about how to ensure your will is valid.

Who should the witnesses be?

It is extremely important that the witnesses must not benefit from the will. Someone who is a beneficiary, or who is married to or the civil partner of a beneficiary, can not be a witness either. If someone you have left a legacy to in your will then witnesses it, this part of the will will not be valid and they would lose their entitlement to their inheritance. The rest of the will would still be valid.

What should you do with your will once you've written it?

There are no rules about where your will should be kept – the important things are that it is somewhere safe where it won't get lost, damaged, or stolen, and that the relevant people know where it is. If you want to check your will every now and then, to be sure it is up to date, you may want to keep it where you can access it easily or keep a copy at home. Wherever you keep it, make sure you tell the executors where it is and make sure they can access it when they need to after your death. You should also tell close friends and family that you have made a will and where it can be found.

If you have used a solicitor to draft your will, they will usually provide a will storage service. Most solicitors won't charge you for storing a will that they have written, even if they are not your executor, and they are required to have secure facilities for storage.

Will writers may also provide this service but, as they are not regulated in the same way as solicitors, they may not have secure facilities in place. It is also important that they have in place some provision for what will happen to wills in their keeping if their business closes down. Check whether they will charge you for storage and how much; they may be offering an attractive charge for drafting the will but the cost of storage could mean you end up paying much more in the long run.

You can also lodge your will at a bank or with another solicitor. Alternatively, you can lodge your will with the High Court for particularly safe keeping. Simply take your will along to your local probate registry to lodge it or contact the Record Keeper's Department at the Principal Registry, First Avenue House in London (see chapter 9 for details). The fee for this is currently £15.

What happens if your circumstances change?

You should review your will every few years to make sure that it still reflects your wishes, and that it is still relevant to your circumstances, in terms of the size and nature of your estate and the people you wish to leave it to. Remember that if you have a will this overrides any informal promises you may have made that aren't mentioned in the will. Before you make your will you should consider whether possible future events might affect the decisions you make and see if you can cover likely changes when you write it. However careful you are though, there could well be changes that will mean that it would be a good idea to update your will.

Marriage or civil partnership

If you get married, or register a civil partnership, any will you made before this will automatically be revoked, this means it will no longer be valid. This is the case unless, when you made it, you expected the marriage to go ahead and you stated that the will is made in contemplation of your marriage, naming your partner (it's important that you have someone specific in mind). If your will doesn't include this kind of clause, you must make a new will taking into account your change of circumstances.

Divorce

If you get divorced, or have a civil partnership annulled, any reference in your will to your former partner will no longer be valid. The will as a whole will not be revoked, the other provisions will still be effective, but if your spouse or civil partner was appointed as executor or a beneficiary this will no longer apply. It is therefore possible that there would be a partial intestacy (i.e. part of your estate would be left unaccounted for) or, if there was no alternative executor named, someone would have to apply to be **administrator**.

Note that the rules are different in Scotland where marriage, civil partnership or divorce do not automatically affect the validity of a will.

Moving into a care home

If you move into a care home, you may decide to sell your home or use up some of your savings paying the care fees and have less left to leave in your will. If the council pays for your care under a deferred payment arrangement, you may have a charge put on your house which would have to be repaid when it is eventually sold. Any of these situations would mean your estate would be lower in value at your death than you might have previously planned for.

Moving abroad

If you move abroad, or buy property abroad, check if your will would still be valid and could deal with any overseas property. It may be necessary to make a will in the country where you own property, as well as one that is valid in England and Wales. This can be a particularly complicated area and you should take legal advice on it.

Changing people

You may want to change your will to include new family members or new friends. For example, you should check whether the will is drafted in a way which includes any new grandchildren.

If any of the people you have chosen as executors die before you, you may have to change your will to replace them, unless when it is drafted it provides for a replacement. It may also be necessary to change your will if one of the beneficiaries dies before you, especially if it was the person to whom you had left the residuary legacy (the remainder of your estate after all specific gifts have been made). Unless you have named a replacement beneficiary, this is likely to result in a partial intestacy.

The changing value of your estate

If you have left specific sums of money to people, over time these will drop in value as the cost of living rises. Also, if the value of your estate rises significantly, for example if you inherit a substantial gift yourself, you may want to increase the sums that you leave to others.

If you have left specific legacies (for example for your piano to go to your brother, or a particular piece of furniture to go to your niece) and you have since sold these items, these beneficiaries will lose out, unless you have provided for this possibility in some way in your will.

How can you change your will?

If you decide you need to change your will, you have two options:

i) You can write an amendment or addition to your will as a separate document, (called a **codicil**) which is then kept with the original will. This is really only suitable for minor amendments.

ii) Alternatively, you can revoke your will and create a new one.

Which of these options is the most appropriate will depend on how significant the changes are that you wish to make.

Making a codicil

A codicil could be suitable for a simple amendment such as replacing an executor or deleting a particular provision that has no bearing on the rest of the will. You can use more than one codicil but, because a series of codicils making multiple amendments is likely to cause confusion and complication, it would usually be better to make a new will.

An example of when a codicil might be useful is if you have left some money to the children of a friend and that friend then has another child, you could use a codicil to add the name of the new baby to your will. This should be a simple addition which wouldn't affect the rest of the will.

Similarly, if you have second thoughts about the reliability of someone you've named as executor, you could amend your will simply by replacing their name with that of someone else. Again, this is the kind of simple amendment for which a codicil might be appropriate.

You must not write or make any mark on the original will; the amendment must be made in the codicil which is a separate document.

A codicil must be signed and witnessed in the same way as a will, so you will need to sign it in front of two witnesses who must also then sign it. Just as with the original will, the witnesses must not be beneficiaries under the will (even if the codicil doesn't affect those particular beneficiaries).

If you use a codicil, you must make sure it does not get separated from the original will.

Do not staple or clip anything other than a codicil to your will. If some other document is attached and then removed, the marks left behind could suggest that there was a codicil that has been lost and could raise doubts about the validity of the will.

Making a new will

If you make a new will, it must start by saying that it revokes all previous wills (this makes it clear you want to cancel your previous will). In order to actually revoke the old will, you must physically destroy it – burn it or tear it up rather than just putting a cross through it. If you have previously used a codicil, you must also destroy the codicil.

You should make sure that the people who knew about your original will know you have made a new one. And if you have named new executors, you should make sure that the executors under your old will know that they have been replaced. This should help to avoid any confusion or dispute when the new executors need to take up their role.

It may not cost as much to make a new will if it is largely the same as your old one.

Summary

There are a number of reasons why your will may need to be updated at some point. Don't let the fact that things may change put you off making a will: it can be a simple matter to change it. You could see making your will as an ongoing process, and you should be aware that, when significant changes occur in your life this might require significant changes to your will. There's no point making a will if by the time it comes into effect it no longer does what you wanted it to.

5

Lasting Powers of Attorney and advance decisions

So far in this book, we have looked at how you can make plans to ensure your wishes are carried out after your death and that things are made easier for the people left behind. This chapter looks at other ways you might want to plan for your future in case there is a time when you can't make certain decisions for yourself. The options looked at here are lasting powers of attorney and **advance decisions** (sometimes called **living wills**):

- A Lasting Power of Attorney (or 'LPA') allows you to choose someone to make decisions on your behalf.
- An advance decision records your wish to refuse a certain type of medical treatment in the future.

The reasons for taking the steps set out in this chapter are the same as for making a will, namely to make things easier for those close to you and to make sure your wishes are carried out if you aren't able to say what you want.

The measures discussed in this chapter are governed by the Mental Capacity Act 2005 which only applies to England and Wales. The law is different in Scotland and Northern Ireland and this is not dealt with in this book. Chapter 9 gives details of where you can go for information on the position in Scotland and Northern Ireland.

When might you be unable to make decisions for yourself?

People may lose **mental capacity** to make their own decisions for a number of reasons, for example it could be due to an accident, stroke, or dementia. It can also cover very temporary situations such as if you are unconscious while having an operation. To have mental capacity to make a decision, you must be able to understand and retain the information relevant to the decision, understand the implications and be able to communicate the decision. You may have capacity to make some decisions but not others, and capacity will often fluctuate, so you may have good days when you are able to make your own decisions and bad days when you are not.

It's important to remember that dementia is not an inevitable part of getting old and it won't be an issue for the large majority of people. But because you never know what will happen to you in the future, it is worth considering arrangements to help your family know what you would want to happen if you were unable to tell them.

Mental Capacity Act principles

The Mental Capacity Act sets out principles to be followed when dealing with someone who may lack capacity to make a particular decision. The principles aim to make sure everyone makes their own decisions if possible and, if not, show how others should make decisions on their behalf. If you make an LPA, your attorney must also follow these principles.

1. A person must be assumed to have capacity unless it is proved otherwise.
2. All practicable steps must be taken to help someone make their own decisions before anyone concludes they are unable to do so.
3. A person is not to be treated as unable to make a decision simply because they have made an unwise decision.
4. Any action taken or decision made on behalf of someone who lacks capacity must be in their best interests.
5. Before an action is taken or decision made on behalf of someone who lacks capacity, all effective alternatives must be considered with regard to which is the least restrictive of the person's rights and freedom of action.

Lasting Powers of Attorney (LPA)

An LPA is a way of appointing someone else to make decisions on your behalf. This person is then known as your **attorney** (see below). There are two different types of LPA. Both are a way of authorising someone else to make decisions for you, but one concerns decisions around your finances and the other is about your health and welfare:

- Your property and financial affairs: You can create a property and affairs LPA to give one or more people (your attorneys) the authority to handle your financial affairs and property. This could cover decisions such as paying your bills, investing your money or selling your property. You can chose to have a property and affairs LPA that can be used to allow someone to handle your affairs even when you still have the mental capacity to do so yourself. You may want to do this if, for example, you have physical difficulty with organising things yourself or if you just want someone else to be able to help out. Alternatively, you can specify that it can only be used if you lose mental capacity.

- Your health and personal welfare: A personal welfare LPA gives your attorney, or attorneys, power to make decisions on your behalf about your health, care and personal welfare, but only if you do not have the mental capacity to do so yourself. This could cover decisions such as what medical treatment you would not want to receive, where you should live or who you should have contact with. If you are able to make these decisions yourself, you must do so; your attorney can only make decisions which you lack capacity to make yourself.

Both types of LPA must be registered with the **Office of the Public Guardian** (OPG) before they can be used (see chapter 9 for contact details).

There is a charge for registration. This is currently £120 for each LPA (this fee is subject to change so you should check with the OPG), so if you are registering both a property and affairs LPA and a personal welfare LPA it will cost a total of £300 (see later in this chapter for information on how to make and register a LPA).

LPAs replaced the previous system of enduring powers of attorney (EPAs). If you have already made an EPA, you can still use it, as long as it was created before 1st October 2007, even if it hasn't yet been registered (but it must be registered if you lose mental capacity). EPAs only cover financial decisions, so you might want to consider making an LPA for personal welfare decisions as well.

Why make an LPA?

If you have an LPA in place, it makes the practicalities of dealing with your affairs much easier, should it be necessary for decisions to be made on your behalf. For example, you may need someone to pay your bills on time, to make decisions about where you should be cared for and to make arrangements to pay for your care if necessary. An LPA is proof (for example to show to your bank) that the person named as your attorney has your authority to act for you.

If no one has been given that authority through an LPA, or EPA, it may be necessary for someone to make an application to the **Court of Protection**.

This is the court with power to make decisions on the affairs of people who lack mental capacity. The Court can give someone authority to act on your behalf (called a **Deputy**) but making an LPA allows you to make that choice yourself, and avoids the cost and delay involved in making an application to the Court.

Decisions about your care and treatment if you haven't made an LPA

The personal welfare LPA is an entirely new arrangement, introduced in October 2007. If you don't make a personal welfare LPA, and you lose mental capacity to make those decisions, it will be the people responsible for your care and medical treatment who make decisions about your personal welfare. They must follow the principles of the Mental Capacity Act (see earlier in this chapter) when making decisions and so all decisions must be made in your best interests. If there is disagreement over what is in your best interests, the Court of Protection can make a decision on this.

When deciding what is in your best interests, the person making the decision (for example the doctor providing your treatment) has a duty to consult with your family, carers and others close to you, in order to make an informed decision. They must also take into account any statements that you have made indicating your wishes. This kind of statement can be legally binding if it is an advance decision to refuse certain treatment (see page 58 for more on advance decisions).

Decisions about life-sustaining treatment

If you are creating a personal welfare LPA, you must indicate on the form whether or not you wish to give your attorney authority to make a decision refusing life-sustaining medical treatment for you, even if refusing treatment puts your life is at risk. Your LPA form won't be valid if you don't make this decision, so you can't miss out this part of the form. This is clearly something you should consider carefully. If you don't give your attorney this authority, decisions about life-sustaining treatment will be made by the people providing that treatment, in your best interests. They should consult with your attorney and others close to you when deciding what is in your best interests, but your attorney will not have the final decision unless you say this in your LPA.

Who to choose as your attorney

Deciding who to appoint as your attorney, or attorneys, is an extremely important part of creating an LPA. You must be absolutely sure you can trust them to act in your best interests. People usually choose a relative or friend to be their attorney. You should also make sure that they are prepared to take on the role and that they understand the responsibility involved.

You can appoint more than one attorney. If you do, you should try to choose people who will be able to work together without too many disagreements, but who will check that the other is always acting in your best interests.

If you create both a personal welfare LPA and a property and affairs LPA, you can choose to have the same person responsible for both but you should be aware these are two very different roles.

Your property and financial affairs attorney: Your property and affairs attorney should be someone with sufficient skills and financial understanding to be able to handle your affairs. The amount of skill needed will depend on the complexity of your finances. If you just need someone who can pay your bills and spend your money to meet your needs, it should be enough that you can see they handle their own money well. If they will be dealing with complex investments, you may want someone with more expertise.

Your health and personal welfare attorney: Your personal welfare attorney should be someone who knows you well and who understands your beliefs and values. They should know about your preferences and opinions, so that they can make decisions in your best interests, taking into account the kinds of decisions you have made yourself in the past. If you have strong feelings about a particular type of treatment you should make sure they are aware of and understand this.

How to make an LPA

You can obtain the form and various free guidance booklets from the Office of the Public Guardian. You can complete it yourself if you are confident that you understand the nature and effect of an LPA, you don't want to include any complex restrictions on the power of your attorney and you have the time and patience to go through the guidance documents that accompany the form. Otherwise, you should get advice from a solicitor or advice agency.

The LPA form is much longer than the old EPA form, partly because some safeguards have been added in to try to prevent fraud and abuse of the system. There is always a risk that people may be put under undue pressure to appoint someone to handle their affairs who may use the power for their own gain.

One of the new safeguards is that the LPA form must be signed by someone who can certify that you understand the purpose and effect of the LPA and that you have not been put under any pressure to create it. This **certificate provider** can be a suitably qualified professional, such as a GP or solicitor, or someone who has known you for at least two years but is not a member of your family or your attorney.

In addition, the form includes space for you to name up to five people who will be notified when an application is made to register the LPA. These people can object to the registration of the LPA if they have any concerns that it will be misused.

Because the LPA form takes longer than the old EPA form to fill out, solicitors may charge more than previously to help. However it is not essential to use a solicitor when creating an LPA; there is plenty of guidance available on how to complete the form yourself.

Before sending off your LPA form for registration, check, double check and triple check that all required parts have been properly completed. The Office of the Public Guardian can and does refuse to register incomplete forms, even if it is what appears to be a minor mistake such as forgetting to tick a required box. If your form is returned as invalid, you will have to submit a new one, and pay another registration fee.

When to register the LPA

Your LPA cannot be used until it has been registered with the Office of the Public Guardian (see chapter 9 for contact details). This will take a minimum of six weeks, as the OPG must give people time to object to the registration if they have concerns about fraud or abuse. You can either register the LPA yourself once you have created it, whilst you still have mental capacity to do so or your attorney can register it when it is needed.

Reasons to register your LPA straight away:

- If you wait until it is needed, there will be a delay before your attorney can act on your behalf. If it is necessary for important decisions to be taken during this time, an emergency application to the Court of Protection may be required.
- If any mistakes have been made on the form, or the OPG thinks your instructions to your attorney are not clear enough, you can amend them. If the mistakes are only discovered when you no longer have capacity to make decisions about your LPA, it may not be possible to register it.

Reasons for delaying registration until your LPA is needed:

- It is quite likely that you will never need the LPA to be used as most people will never reach a point when they are unable to make decisions for themselves. Delaying registration could save you the registration fee if it turns out that you never need it. This could of course turn out to be a false economy if the delay means the unregistered LPA is no use to you in an emergency.

Advance decisions
What is an advance decision?

An advance decision is sometimes known as a living will. Like a will it is a statement of your wishes, but it is very specific and only covers a decision that you do not want a particular type of medical treatment to be given to you in the future, if you are unable to make or communicate that decision at the time.

In general, everyone has the right to refuse any medical treatment for any reason, but you do not have the right to demand to have any particular medical treatment as this may conflict with the professional opinion of those treating you. Usually you would be able to discuss your treatment with those providing your care and, if you decide to refuse the treatment, you can explain this to them. They are bound to respect your decision, even if the withdrawal of treatment could lead to your death.

An advance decision can be used to make sure that you can still exercise your right to refuse treatment even when you are unconscious or lack mental capacity and it is legally binding on those providing your care.

Why make an advance decision?

People often make advance decisions after they have been diagnosed with a progressive illness or dementia and they are thinking about how any future treatment might affect their quality of life. An advance decision is often used to indicate that someone does not want life-sustaining treatment which they feel would not result in the quality of life they would want. Planning for a time like this obviously involves difficult decisions and an advance decision is not going to be the right option for everyone.

An advance decision can also be appropriate if you have strong feelings about a particular type of treatment. This could be because it conflicts with your beliefs and values, for example some people would not want a blood transfusion in any circumstances.

Making an advance decision is a good opportunity to discuss aspects of your future care with people who are close to you. It will raise issues that are important but difficult to talk about, particularly if you are considering whether you would want to refuse certain treatments that could prolong your life. Discussing this with your family and friends could make it easier for them if a decision about such treatment does have to be made in the future and, particularly if you do decide to refuse such treatment, to understand your reasons for doing so.

If you make an advance decision and then later create a personal welfare LPA giving your attorney power to refuse medical treatment on your behalf, your advance decision will no longer be valid. You should discuss your views on treatment with your attorney, as it will be for them to make the decision taking into account your past wishes, if you are unable to do so yourself. Alternatively you could state on your LPA that your attorney does not have authority to make decisions about refusing medical treatment, in which case your advance decision will still be valid.

How to make a legally binding advance decision

There is no standard form that must be used for an advance decision. If you are refusing treatment where your life is not at risk, an advance decision can be valid even if it is only made verbally as long as you had mental capacity to make it at the time. An advance decision only has to be in writing, signed and witnessed if it is a decision to refuse life-sustaining treatment (see later in this chapter).

However, there are obvious risks with only making a verbal statement: the people providing your treatment may not be aware that you have made it and it may not be clear enough for them to be sure it is applicable to the particular situation. If they are not sure that a valid advance decision exists, the doctor can go ahead and provide the treatment.

The wording should be clear enough so that there is no uncertainty about which treatment and circumstances it will apply to. You should state what type of treatment you wish to refuse, and in what circumstances, giving as much detail as possible. You should also include a statement that the decision is to apply if you lack mental capacity to make the decision yourself at the relevant time. It is also a good idea to get someone to witness your signature on the document.

Putting your advance decision in writing, telling family and friends that you have made it, letting your doctor know about it and perhaps keeping a copy with your medical records will help to avoid any uncertainty about its validity.

You might find it helpful to discuss your advance decision with your doctor, so that you have a full understanding of the potential treatments that may be proposed in the future and the consequences of refusing them. Your doctor should be able to help with the wording you should use to avoid uncertainty when describing the treatment you would refuse and the situations in which you would refuse it. You could also ask your doctor, or another suitable person, to sign the advance decision confirming that, in their opinion, you understood the purpose and effect of making the decision at the time you made it.

Advance decisions to refuse life-sustaining treatment

There are special rules for advance decisions to refuse treatment that is necessary to keep you alive. Life-sustaining treatment can include, for example, artificial nutrition and hydration for people who are unable to eat or drink by mouth. The rules for creating an advance decision to refuse this kind of treatment are stricter, for obvious reasons:

- The decision must be recorded in writing.
- You must sign it (or instruct someone to sign it on your behalf if you can't do so yourself).
- Your signature must be witnessed and the witness must also sign the document in your presence.
- The document must include a written statement that it is to apply to the treatment even if your life is at risk.

The Alzheimer's Society produces a form to create an advance decision to refuse life-sustaining treatment (see chapter 9 for details of how to obtain this). Before using it, or any other standard form, you should carefully consider whether the wording used fully reflects your own personal decision. You may prefer to use the form as an example and amend the wording so that it reflects your own situation. You could discuss the exact wording with your doctor.

What is an advance statement?

The term living will is also sometimes used to refer to an advance statement, but it is important to realise that this is different from an advance decision. An advance statement is a statement indicating your wishes relating to anything else other than refusal of treatment. So it indicates what you would like to ask for, rather than what you would like to refuse. This must be taken into account by the people responsible for decisions about your care, but it is not legally binding on them. An advance statement does not have to be about medical treatment, for example it could be about your dietary preferences. If you lose capacity to decide what you should eat, the person responsible for providing your food, whether it is a family member or professional carer, must consider your statement and this should influence their decision when deciding what kind of diet is in your best interests.

Keeping your advance decision up to date

If there have been developments that you had not anticipated at the time you made your decision, such as new developments in medical treatment or changes in your personal circumstances, the people treating you are entitled to decide that had you known about this you may have reached a different decision. In these circumstances, they can go against your decision and provide the treatment.

Bearing this in mind you should review your advance decision from time to time, and sign and date it again to confirm it is still an accurate indication of your wishes.

Summary

A Lasting Power of Attorney will not be a suitable option for everyone. There may be no one who you would want to give the authority to act on your behalf and you may prefer to leave it to the relevant people (such as your doctor, or carer, or the Court of Protection) to make decisions in your best interests if the time comes. Whether or not to make an LPA is a personal decision but one which should be made with a proper understanding of how an LPA could work and what might happen if you don't make one. The same is true, perhaps to a greater extent, with advanced decisions; it is not a step everyone would want to take or needs to take. But again, a good understanding of the issues and practicalities will help you make the right choice.

If you decide not to make these arrangements, you might still want to talk to people close to you about how you would feel about certain decisions that could be necessary on your behalf in the future. They may be involved with those decisions and can help paint a picture of what would be in your best interests.

6

Inheritance tax

What is inheritance tax?

Inheritance tax (IHT) is a tax that may apply when you give away money or assets. Below we look at when it would have to be paid out of the estate after your death (it is sometimes payable during your lifetime but this isn't dealt with in this book). If you think this may apply to you we recommend you seek professional advice.

Despite the amount of press coverage it gets most people don't have to worry about IHT, the value of most people's estates is not high enough for IHT to be payable at all. In 2007/08 IHT had to be paid on only 6% of estates in the UK. This is expected to fall to even fewer people in the future due to changes in the rules on transferring a tax-free amount between spouses or civil partners (see below for more on this).

You will only have to pay IHT if your **taxable estate** is worth more than the **IHT threshold** (this is £325,000 for the tax year 2009/10). Taxable estate means the amount of your estate that counts for IHT purposes: this may be different from the value of your actual estate because some things in your estate are exempt from IHT and some things that you no longer have when you die, such as sums of money you have recently given away, may still count as part of your taxable estate.

If what you have, including the value of your house, is way below £325,000, you can skip this chapter. If, though, you are above or near this £325,000 then you may want to look at what you can do to minimise the amount that tax would have to be paid on.

How to calculate how much IHT might have to be paid on an estate

Understanding the basics of how IHT is calculated can help you plan to minimise the tax that will eventually be payable or could put your mind at rest by confirming that it is unlikely that IHT will be payable at all.

In order to know whether IHT is payable on an estate, and if so how much, you need to calculate the following:

- The total value of your estate, minus any tax-free gifts made in your will, plus the running total of gifts made in the seven years before your death.
- IHT is payable if the total is higher than the IHT threshold (i.e. £325,000 in 2009/10) and it is only payable on the amount you have above the threshold.
- The rate for IHT paid on your estate after your death is currently 40% of the value above the threshold.

Estimating the total value of your estate

Your estate means all your property, possessions, cash and investments, minus any money you owe at the time of your death. The value of the estate is calculated by using the 'market value' of assets at the date of your death (i.e. what you can sell them for, not what you paid for them).

Tax-free gifts made in your will

Certain types of gifts made in your will are tax free, so they don't count towards the final total of your taxable estate. When calculating whether IHT is payable, the value of any of the following types of gift is deducted from the total value of your estate:

- Anything you leave to your spouse or civil partner (but note that if your spouse or civil partner lives abroad the exemption relating to gifts between spouses or civil partners is limited to £55,000).
- Gifts to a charity.
- Gifts to a political party.
- Gifts to particular national institutions, museums, galleries or universities.
- Other gifts for the 'public benefit'. Gifts of works of art, or other national heritage property, could be exempt depending on, among other things, who you give them to and whether they agree to allow public access to the works.
- Gifts to a housing association.
- Gifts of agricultural land with vacant possession.

Your business: If part of your estate is made up of your own business, or a share in a partnership, business property relief may apply if you pass this on as a gift under your will. This can mean that no IHT is payable on the gift of your business.

Lump sums from pension schemes or life insurance policies: If these are nominated or written in trust, they do not form part of your estate and so are not taxable. You might want to get legal advice about this.

Gifts made during your lifetime

It is not just the value of your estate at the date of your death which is relevant for IHT purposes: gifts made in the seven years before your death are also taken into account. This is so that someone cannot avoid paying IHT by giving away their property and possessions before their death.

There are many exemptions relating to IHT which mean that it is not payable on all gifts or transfers.

The 'nil-rate band'

The Government sets the threshold above which IHT is payable and this generally goes up every year. The thresholds have already been announced for the years up until 2011. For the tax year 2009/10 it is £325,000 and for 2010/11 it is £350,000 (the tax year runs from 6th April to 5th April). The relevant threshold is the current one at the date of death, not at the date of payment of tax.

IHT is only payable on the amount of the estate that is over the threshold. Anything below the threshold falls within what is called the **nil-rate band** (i.e. 'nil' IHT is payable on it). So in a basic example of someone who died on 1st May 2009 with a taxable estate worth £350,000, the first £325,000 of the estate would fall within the nil-rate band, so IHT would be payable on the last £25,000 at 40%. The IHT bill would therefore be £10,000.

Transfer of the unused nil-rate band

Since 9th October 2007, it has been possible for any unused part of your nil-rate band to be transferred to your spouse or civil partner. So in effect it is possible for some people to double their nil-rate band.

Part of the nil-rate band would be unused if, for example, the total estate was not worth enough for IHT to be payable or if someone left the whole of their estate to their spouse or civil partner. In this last example, as no IHT is payable on anything left to a spouse or civil partner, regardless of the value of the estate, none of the nil-rate band is used.

When the second spouse or civil partner dies, the proportion of the first partner's allowance that was not used will be added to their own nil-rate band allowance. This means that, along with what you inherit from your husband or wife, you also inherit any 'unused' tax-free allowance that is then added to your tax-free allowance when you die. The new rules apply where the second spouse or civil partner dies on or after 9th October 2007. It does not matter when the death of the first person occurred. Even if the death occurred before the introduction of IHT in 1986, the unused proportion of the nil-rate band applicable under the old systems of either estate duty or capital transfer tax can be transferred over.

Liaquat dies in 2009, when the nil-rate band is £325,000. He leaves everything to his wife Asma. Although the value of his estate was above the threshold for tax to be payable, no tax was due because the exemption for transfers between spouses applied. 100% of his nil-rate band remains unused. So on Asma's death her nil-rate band will effectively double. If she dies in 2010, when the nil-rate band is £350,000, IHT will only be payable on her estate if it is worth over £700,000.

It is the *proportion* of the nil-rate band that was unused that is transferred over, not the *value in pounds* at the time of the first death.

Thomas died in 1996, leaving a widow, Julia. Thomas left £50,000 to his daughter, and the rest to Julia. It was therefore only the amount he left to his daughter that counted when adding up the value of his estate for IHT purposes. The nil-rate band in 1996 at the time of his death was £200,000, so although no IHT was payable on what he left his daughter, the £50,000 used up 25% of his nil-rate band, leaving 75% of it unused. This 'tax-free' allowance would now be 'transferred' to his wife so that on Julia's death, her nil-rate band is increased by 75%. If the nil-rate band at the time of Julia's death has risen to £325,000, she has her own £325,000 allowance, plus £243,750 (75% of £325,000) from her husband's unused IHT tax-free allowance. Her total nil-rate band will therefore be £568,750. If the value of her estate is worth less than £568,750, no IHT will be payable.

The nil-rate bands going back to 1914 are available on HMRC website or by calling the Probate and Inheritance Tax Helpline on Tel: 0845 302 0900.

Responsibility for claiming the transferred nil-rate band lies with the **personal representative** (i.e. the executor or administrator) of the second spouse or civil partner to die. Chapter 8 looks at the role of the personal representative in paying IHT.

Planning to minimise IHT

If you find, having added up your taxable estate, that there might be IHT to pay on your estate, you may want to consider ways to minimise this.

Always keep in mind that minimising tax is not your only aim when planning your estate. You need to make sure that your estate benefits the people and organisations you want it to, even if this means more tax is paid. For example, if you chose to leave your whole estate to a charity or political party, you would have successfully avoided any IHT being payable but your family and friends may not be impressed with your planning if they had expected to inherit from you. They may have preferred to have received a smaller inheritance after tax rather than receive nothing at all. So whilst leaving money to charity in your will is clearly a very positive thing to do, it shouldn't be done solely for tax reasons if the result is that other potential beneficiaries lose out.

Similarly, giving away your money and property during your lifetime can be a way of reducing the IHT payable on your death but it means you will have less to live on until you do die.

The main way for people with a spouse or civil partner to minimise IHT used to be to make sure that they both used their nil-rate band. This is no longer as relevant as an unused nil-rate band can now as already explained be transferred to a spouse or civil partner. Solicitors and accountants often advised setting up something called a **discretionary trust** *to minimise the IHT, or that part of the estate of the first partner to die should be left directly to the children, so that all of the nil-rate band could be used. If your will includes such provisions, you should take advice as to whether this is still the best way to plan your estate.*

Below are some things you could do which may reduce your IHT liability. They are not recommended for everyone and remember they are only worth considering if you may have to pay IHT. You should take advice about the effects and risks of any of these measures if you are not sure.

Make your will

Making a will is a big part of planning to minimise tax. In chapter 1 we looked at reasons for making a will and the consequences of not doing so. If IHT is likely to be relevant to you, there is even more reason to get professional advice, including financial advice, on the most effective way of drafting your will. It would be very unwise to try doing this yourself, unless you have the professional expertise required.

Use your allowances

Using your lifetime tax-free gift allowances means that you can reduce the value of your estate and less tax will be payable. The first £3,000 worth of gifts you make each year is ignored for IHT purposes and, in addition, all gifts of £250 or less to any one person in a year are exempt. You can also make regular gifts of any amount as long as they are out of your income (this means they come out of your wages, pension or interest on savings etc. and do not reduce the capital value of your estate).

These gifts will not be taken into account even if you die within seven years of making the gifts. Of course this is only sensible if you can afford to do it and still have enough for your own needs.

Beware of making gifts but retaining some kind of benefit, for example giving your house to your children but retaining the right to live in it rent free until your death. These are called gifts with reservation and will be included as part of your taxable estate.

Get professional financial and legal advice to make sure your tax planning ideas will be effective and lawful.

Get married or enter a civil partnership

Obviously you don't want to let your desire to avoid IHT cloud your judgment here. But if you're intending to leave an estate which is liable to IHT to your partner and you've perhaps been thinking of getting married or registering a civil partnership anyway, IHT reduction may be the deciding factor (if not the most romantic one).

You could also look at it that you're giving your family and friends the chance to indulge in some of their own IHT planning – wedding gifts up to certain amounts are exempt from IHT. Parents can give up to £5,000 without it counting towards their taxable estate, grandparents can give up to £2,500 and for anyone else up to £1,000 is exempt. So you might want to remind your friends of the opportunity to buy you an IHT-free wedding gift of up to £1,000.

Set up a trust

There may be a way that you could make use of a trust scheme such as a loan trust or discounted gift trust. Both of these allow you to continue to receive an income from the assets you transfer, so you will still have money to live on. Get professional advice as to whether either of these options is appropriate for you. If you have any life insurance policies, these should be written into trust. This means the benefit would be paid directly to the beneficiary, without forming part of your estate and IHT would not be payable on it. The monthly premium would be a regular gift out of your income and would be exempt.

Invest in a private business

You can make use of business relief by investing in shares listed on the Alternative Investment Market or unquoted shares in a privately owned company. These are free of IHT after you have held them for two years. You could either leave the shares to a beneficiary or they could be sold after your death and the value would form part of your estate to be distributed. Seek advice from an independent financial adviser and be sure you understand the risks involved with this kind of investment.

Insurance

Another option is to take out an insurance policy to pay out on your death to cover an IHT bill. While this isn't strictly a way of reducing the tax itself, it could mean more of your estate goes to your beneficiaries. You can take out a whole life insurance policy specifically for this purpose. Again, seek advice before doing this.

Deed of variation

If you die and there is IHT payable, it may not necessarily be too late: in limited circumstances your will can be changed after your death in order to minimise IHT payable. This can be done within two years of your death but only if none of the legacies have already been distributed and all beneficiaries agree. The important thing is that everyone entitled to benefit under the existing will must agree to the new terms. If a beneficiary feels they would be disadvantaged, or that it would go against the wishes of the person who made the will, the terms of the will cannot be changed. This is an option for your beneficiaries and executors after your death, if they all agree there would have been a better way of arranging things under the will but it shouldn't be necessary if you have planned your estate effectively.

A deed of variation can even be entered into when someone has died intestate. If the people entitled to the estate under the intestacy rules (see chapter 1) all agree, the distribution of the estate can be altered to make it more tax efficient.

Summary

Whilst IHT seems to be a particularly unpopular tax, it's actually something that most of us shouldn't have to worry about at all. This should now be the case for even more people, due to the new rules on the transfer of the nil-rate band. Even if it is relevant for you, with a bit of forward planning there are steps you can take now to minimise the amount that will eventually be payable on your estate. If in any doubt, seek legal and financial advice.

7

What to do when someone dies

This chapter deals briefly with the first steps to take after someone has died, including how to register a death, how to locate a will and dealing with bereavement. You may find it useful if a close relative or friend dies or if you want to help your family and friends be prepared for what to do in the event of your death.

This isn't intended to cover everything you need to know in this event, but should point you in the right direction for getting more information and support if you need it.

Registering a death

When someone dies, the death should be registered within five days (or within eight days if the death occurred in Scotland). The Registrar can give permission for this period to be extended in some circumstances, and so you should contact the **register office** as soon as possible if there could be a delay. It should usually be a relative of the person who has died who registers the death. If there are no relatives available someone else can do it, such as someone present at the death, a hospital official if the person died in hospital or the person arranging the funeral.

You can go to any register office to provide the information needed to register the death but, if you go to one in a different area to where the death occurred, it may take longer to get the certificates. To find the address of the register office, you can search at *www.gro.gov.uk*, look in your local phone book or call *0151 471 4805*.

If the person who has died was visited by a doctor within the 14 days before their death that doctor will provide two certificates: a medical certificate showing the cause of death and a formal notice stating that they have signed the medical certificate. You will need to take both of these certificates to the register office.

If the person who has died had not been seen by a doctor within 14 days before their death, or if the cause of death is unknown or unnatural, the death will be referred to the Coroner. The registration cannot then go ahead until the Coroner has completed his or her investigation.

As well as the two certificates from the doctor, you will have to provide the registrar with information about the person who has died such as their last address, the date and place of their birth, the date and place of their death and details of their spouse or civil partner if they had one. If possible you should also take their NHS medical card, birth certificate and marriage/civil partnership certificate if they had one. But you shouldn't delay registering the death if you can't find these.

The death certificate

You can buy copies of the death certificate when you register the death (you won't be given a free one). You, or whoever is dealing with the estate, will probably need more than one official copy as you may have to provide them at various stages, for example when claiming on an insurance policy or obtaining the release of funds from a bank. You will also need an official copy if you need to obtain **probate**. You can buy extra copies at a later date from the register office or by ordering them online, by phone or by post. It may be more expensive to buy copies at a later date than at the time of registration. The registrar will also give you a certificate for cremation and burial, and a certificate of registration of death, but this is for dealing with social security benefits and is not the same as a death certificate.

Finding the will

The person who died may have left instructions with their will about their wishes for the funeral, or what they want to happen after their death, so it's important not to leave it too late to look for it.

Even if you think they didn't make a will, you should take steps to find out if there is a will you didn't know about. Ask anyone who they may have talked to about making a will to find out if one exists and where it might be.

They may have kept all their important papers together in one place. If nothing can be found in their home you should contact their solicitor, if they had one. A will is often stored by the solicitor who drafted it or the will could have been stored by the person's bank.

Wills can also be stored at the High Court Probate Registry. You can search for a will by sending a copy of the death certificate to the Record Keeper's Department (see chapter 9, under The Principal Registry, for contact details).

You should also make steps to find out whether the person who died had a funeral plan. Again, this means searching through their documents and asking anyone to whom they may have mentioned it (see chapter 2 for more information about funeral plans).

If there is a will and an executor is named, but this isn't you, contact the executor so that they can apply for **probate** (see chapter 8) and start to deal with the estate.

Arranging the funeral

You, or whoever is taking responsibility for the funeral, should contact a funeral director soon after the death in order to make the necessary arrangements. If the person had a funeral plan, there will already be a nominated funeral director, so you should check this before taking any action.

Although it's not often done, it is possible to arrange a funeral without a funeral director. For advice on this you can contact the Natural Death Centre (see chapter 9 for details).

You can find details of local funeral directors from the National Association of Funeral Directors (again see chapter 9 for contact details). You could contact a few local firms to compare prices and the service they can provide.

If you are receiving pension credit or certain other benefits, and you are responsible for someone's funeral but will find paying for it difficult, you may be entitled to a Funeral Payment from the Social Fund. This can cover the cost of a simple funeral. You should contact your social security office or a local advice centre such as a Citizens Advice Bureau or Age Concern for more information or help with this.

If the person had a private pension, there could be a lump sum payable on their death to cover the cost of a funeral. Check with their employer or pension provider.

Other organisations you might need to contact

Consider who else apart from family and friends should be informed that someone has died. This may include the person's employer or business associates; their landlord; social services or a private care provider if the person was receiving care services at home.

It may be necessary to inform suppliers of utilities such as gas and electricity or services such as the telephone or television, particularly if the person lived alone and these services are to be cancelled. There may also be contracts to be cancelled such as for a mobile phone or a subscription to a magazine.

If the person who has died had registered a lasting power of attorney, or enduring power of attorney, you (or the attorney, if this is not you) should notify the Office of the Public Guardian of the death, and send them the power of attorney document and a copy of the death certificate. See chapter 5 for information on powers of attorney.

The Department for Work and Pensions produces a guide called What to do after a death in England and Wales. *You should be able to get this from a office or Jobcentre Plus, or you can download it from www.direct.gov.uk. It includes information on arranging the funeral, who to contact after the death and financial help such as benefits for bereaved people. There is an equivalent leaflet,* What to do after a death in Scotland *which you can obtain from a registration office in Scotland or from www.scotland.gov.uk.*

Identity theft

Identity theft is often reported as being an increasing problem and using the identity of someone who has died is one way in which it is carried out. A recent change in the law could make this less of a problem as information will be sent to credit agencies by the General Register Office giving details of deaths occurring each week. This should alert the agencies in the event that someone tries to use the identity of someone who has died to obtain credit.

If you are concerned about someone's identity being used fraudulently, there are extra steps you can take. You can register the details of the person who has died with CIFAS (the fraud prevention service) by calling *0870 010 2091*. There is currently an annual charge of £14.10 for this service. Again this will provide an alert if someone tries to gain credit using the identity.

The risk of fraud is also reduced by removing the name of someone who has died from mailing lists. This should stop them being sent junk mail, such as offers to sign up for credit cards, which could be used fraudulently. You can stop such mail by registering with the Bereavement Register *www.the-bereavement-register.org.uk* or the Mailing Preference Service *www.mpsonline.org.uk/mpsr/*.

Coping with bereavement

There are many things to be done in the days and weeks after the death when you may feel least able to cope. There are people you can turn to for support. Cruse Bereavement Care is a charity with local branches where you can talk to a volunteer on a one-to-one basis (see chapter 9 for contact details). Even if you have friends and family around, you might find it helps to talk to a Cruse volunteer or someone else who provides a similar service. There may be a bereavement support group who you could contact in your local area. Your GP may be able to put you in touch with someone who can help.

Summary

Knowing what to do in the first few days after a death can make a difference both in terms of making it easier for you and also being a great help for others affected by the bereavement even if it is just a matter of knowing where to go for advice and support.

There is support available both for the practical arrangements that have to be carried out and with coping with the bereavement itself.

8

Sorting out someone's estate

Chapter 2 looked at the importance of choosing the right person to be your executor. If there is no executor then an administrator will carry out the role of sorting out your estate when you die. This chapter looks at who can get authority to deal with an estate, what they will need to do to get permission to take on this role and the practicalities of carrying it out.

It helps to understand the legal terminology used when talking about estates, especially if you are going to be dealing with solicitors or other professionals involved in the process. The people with authority to deal with the estate are either executors (if they are named in a will) or administrators (if not named in a will). The joint name for administrators and executors is personal representatives.

The document giving official authority to deal with the estate is either called probate (if given to an executor) or **letters of administration** (if given to an administrator). The joint term used to refer to either type of document is **grant of representation**. It is not always necessary for someone to obtain this official authority; in some circumstances you can deal with someone's estate without being appointed as a personal representative (see below for details of when a grant of representation is not needed).

It is often the personal representative who takes on the arrangements that are required immediately after a death, such as organising the funeral, but this does not have to be the case. Their role is specifically to sort out the estate and it may be more appropriate for someone else to arrange the funeral and other personal matters.

The information in this chapter only applies to England and Wales. For information on what to do if you need a grant of representation for someone who lived in Scotland or Northern Ireland contact your local **probate registry**. There are more suggestions for how to find information on Scotland and Northern Ireland in chapter 9.

Who will deal with the estate
If there is a will

As we saw in chapter 2 a will can name someone to deal with the estate – i.e. the executor. As long as this person is still alive and willing and able to carry out the role at the time of the person's death, the named executors are the ones who will deal with the estate. Up to four executors can be appointed at any one time. If more than one is named, not all of them have to act; an executor can renounce (or turn down) the role if they wish to. It would be for the people named to agree between them whether they will all apply for the grant of representation (if that is needed) and deal with the estate.

It is not necessary for there to be a formal 'reading of the will' by a solicitor. Whether it is necessary to use a solicitor at all is looked at on the next page.

If there isn't a will

If someone dies without leaving a valid will, usually someone must be appointed as administrator to sort out the estate. This will be the person's closest relative, in the following order of priority:

1. Husband, wife or civil partner
2. Children
3. Grandchildren
4. Parents
5. Brothers or sisters
6. Nephews or nieces
7. Half-brothers or half-sisters
8. Grandparents
9. Uncles or aunts

So for example, if you are not married or in a civil partnership, and have no children and you die without making a will, the role of administering your estate would fall to one or both of your parents. If your parents are no longer alive, it would be your brothers or sisters and so on.

If you are the partner of the person who has died, but were not married or in a civil partnership, you are not entitled to apply to be administrator. If there is no relative who can apply, the Treasury

Solicitor will deal with the estate and attempt to trace anyone who is entitled to inherit.

Up to four people can be appointed as administrators.

If there is a will but there are no executors

If there is a will but the named executors are unable or unwilling to act, there are different rules again. If the whole estate has been left to one person, or there is someone named as the beneficiary of the remainder of the estate after all other gifts have been made, that person can apply for the grant of representation to deal with the estate.

Should you get help from a solicitor?

If you are named as executor or entitled to be administrator, you can instruct a solicitor to administer the estate on your behalf. You can also use a solicitor to make the application for the grant of representation. All the solicitor's charges will be paid for out of the estate and these could be substantial. You should bear this in mind when deciding whether to seek professional help or administer the estate yourself.

If the estate is complicated, for example it includes business interests or overseas property or involves setting up and administering a trust, you may need to get professional help. This may not necessarily be from a solicitor: depending on the issue in question, a financial adviser or tax accountant may be more suitable. There are details of how to find professional advisers in chapter 9.

Rather than using a solicitor or another professional to advise on all aspects of administering the estate, you could refer to them for advice on particular points if complications arise. This could help to keep the cost down.

For advice and guidance about the procedure of applying for the grant of representation, staff at the **probate registry** should be able to help, but they cannot give legal advice about the distribution of the estate. Contact details for your local probate registry should be in the local phone book or see chapter 9 for more on how to find them.

As a personal representative, you could be personally liable if the estate is not distributed correctly. If you are in doubt about how to carry out your duties, seek advice.

When is it not necessary to obtain a grant of representation?

It is not always necessary to obtain a grant of representation. If the estate is of low value, or all property is held jointly, it can be possible to obtain and distribute the assets without having formal proof (i.e. the grant of representation document) that you are the person with official authority to do this.

If a relatively small amount of money, usually under £5,000, is held in a bank or building society or in a National Savings account, these institutions might release the money they hold without seeing a grant of representation. You should check with each institution whether they require one and, if not, what documentation they will need before they will release any funds.

For example, an institution holding the deceased's money may ask you to obtain a statutory declaration (instead of a grant of representation); this is a document which you sign in front of a solicitor to declare you are entitled to the money.

There is no fee for obtaining a grant of representation if the estate is worth less than £5,000, so you might find that it is more straightforward and cheaper to obtain a grant rather than meeting the individual institutions' requirements to obtain the money.

If property is held as **joint tenants** (see chapter 2) it will automatically pass to the other owner on the death of one owner. Money in a joint bank account automatically passes to the other joint account holder. If all the deceased's property was held in this way, for example if their estate is made up of a jointly owned house and bank accounts in joint names, it is not necessary to obtain a grant of representation.

If a grant of representation is not needed, you can go ahead and collect in all the assets, pay any debts and distribute the estate.

How does a personal representative carry out their role?

As personal representative (remember this refers to both executors or administrators), the main steps you will have to take, in order, are:

1. Work out what is included in the estate and calculate what the total value of the estate will be
2. Use this to work out if inheritance tax has to be paid and, if so, arrange payment
3. Apply for the grant of representation (either probate or letters of administration), if this is necessary
4. Collect in all assets
5. Pay all the debts
6. Distribute the estate.

How to work out the value of the estate to see if inheritance tax needs to be paid

You will need to have an idea of the 'taxable value' of the estate so that you will know whether inheritance tax must be paid. This is important as you can't obtain the grant of representation and start dealing with the estate until the IHT has been paid.

The taxable value of an estate for inheritance tax purposes is not the same as the total value of the estate, as certain gifts are exempt from IHT and it also includes the value of some things given away during the person's lifetime. See chapter 6 for more on how IHT is calculated.

It may be clear from the beginning that the taxable value of the estate is not going to be over the IHT threshold (£325,000 in 2009/10). If there is any doubt then you will need to draw up a list of the value of everything that forms the estate. This might involve:

• Obtaining a valuation of property or possessions. Items should be valued at the amount for which they could be sold, not at the purchase price or insured price. For example you could get an estate agent to value a house or flat.

- Writing to banks, building societies and insurance companies, informing them that the account or policy holder has died and asking for a final statement or valuation. These steps can be taken before the grant is obtained; it should be enough to explain that you are applying for a grant of representation and to enclose a copy of the death certificate.

- Obtaining a valuation of any shares. You may need professional help with this, from a bank, stockbroker or accountant. You should write to the company in which the shares are held to find out if any dividends are due.

If money is held in a joint account with a spouse or civil partner, this would not count towards the total value of the estate for IHT purposes as it would be covered by the exemption for transfers between spouses or civil partners (see chapter 6). For a joint account held with someone who was not their spouse or civil partner, it will be necessary to value their share. This is the value of their contribution to the account, so if the person who died paid in all the money in the account, the whole balance counts towards the value of their estate. If two joint account holders paid in equal shares, then half of the balance at the date of death counts for IHT purposes.

How to pay IHT
When must the IHT payment be made?
Payment of any IHT owing must be made before the grant of representation can be obtained. This

can present a problem as, without the grant of representation, you won't be able to access the assets and funds that make up the estate which you may well need to pay the IHT bill. To get around this *catch 22* situation, you may need to take out a loan to cover the IHT. Alternatively, some financial institutions may release money under the Inheritance Tax Direct Payment Scheme without the grant being obtained first.

Payment must be made within six months of the end of the month in which the death occurred. So for example, for a death occurring in May, the due date is 30th November. Interest will be charged if payment is not made within the required six months and penalty charges can also be applied if payment is not paid twelve months after the end of the month in which the person died.

You may not have full details of the value of the estate by the time payment is required, so it is possible to pay an estimated amount pending the final calculation. For example, you may have to do this if you are selling property and can't be sure how much it will actually sell for. If you include provisional estimated values on the IHT form, you must inform HM Revenue & Customs (HMRC) as soon as you know the actual value. You can then either pay any shortfall or claim a refund when the total amount payable has been calculated.

IHT on land, buildings or a business can be paid in instalments over a period of ten years. It is only worth doing this for land or buildings if there is not enough cash in the estate to pay it immediately,

as interest is charged. No interest is charged on the delayed payment of IHT relating to a business.

The IHT form: If IHT is payable, you must send form IHT200 to HMRC (the form will tell you where you need to send it). You can either work out the amount payable yourself or they will make the provisional calculation based on the information you give them.

Even if you are asking HMRC to calculate the tax payable, filling in the required parts of IHT200 may not be a straightforward matter. You have to provide all the details to allow them to make the calculation. There are a number of supplementary pages for providing the necessary information, such as details of any gifts made in the last seven years, the value of any household and personal goods, investments and property that makes up the estate. You may want to get help from a solicitor. The cost of this would be paid for out of the estate of the deceased.

How to apply for the transfer of an unused nil-rate band: If the person whose estate you are dealing with had a spouse or civil partner who died before them and who did not use the whole of their nil-rate band, the unused proportion can be transferred. To apply for this to be transferred, you need to send form IHT216 to HMRC at the same time as you send IHT200. If you are making such a claim, you will need documentation relating to the estate of the spouse or civil partner who died first, such as their IHT return, will and death certificate.

If you are the personal representative for someone who dies leaving a surviving spouse or civil partner, if part of the nil-rate band is unused it is important to keep the necessary documentation on this so that it is available at the time of the death of the surviving spouse or civil partner.

Obtaining confirmation that all tax has been paid: Once you know the final value of the estate, you can use form IHT30 to obtain a certificate that all IHT has been paid. Once the certificate is returned to you by HMRC you can be sure that there will not be any further demand for tax and you can finalise the distribution of the estate.

You can get more information and download the IHT forms from www.hmrc.gov.uk or by calling the HMRC Probate and IHT Helpline on 0845 302 0900.

How to obtain the grant of representation

The procedure and the forms required are the same for both types of grant of representation (so it doesn't make any difference if you are an executor or an administrator).

You can use a solicitor to obtain a grant or you can do it yourself. Around 70% of all applications are made through a solicitor; this includes estates where the solicitor has been appointed as executor. If you apply through a solicitor, there is no need to attend a personal interview at the probate registry office; instead, you will have to swear an oath (or make an affirmation) in front of another solicitor. By doing this you are stating that the contents of your application are true.

You will need to complete the probate application form (PA1) and either the form declaring that no IHT is payable on the estate (IHT205) or the form confirming that it has been paid (D18). The death certificate and the original will (with any codicils) should also be enclosed with your probate application. You will also need to enclose a cheque for the application fee. The fee is currently £90 for a standard application but there is no fee where the value of the estate is below £5,000.

You can download the probate application forms from the HMRC website www.hmcs.gov.uk, order them from the Probate and Inheritance Tax Helpline 0845 3020900 or from your local probate registry.

You will be sent an appointment for an interview at the probate registry. There is a probate registry office where interviews can take place in most cities and large towns; you indicate which venue you would like to attend on your application form. At the interview you have to show proof of your identity and swear, or affirm, that the information you have given in your application is correct.

The grant will be posted to you after the interview. The original death certificate will also be returned, but the original will remains at the probate registry and is now a public document.

When you write to institutions like banks to ask for access to the deceased person's finances, you enclose the grant

of representation to prove to them that you have the right to this information. You can send the same copy of the grant to each institution in turn but it is quicker to send separate copies. You cannot use ordinary photocopies of the grant to obtain assets; it has to be an official sealed copy obtained from the probate registry. To speed up the process of collecting in the assets, you can order extra official copies of the grant at the time you submit your application (it's slightly more expensive to do it later).

Collecting in all the assets

Before distributing the estate, you must collect all the assets that form part of the estate. If you have obtained enough official copies of the grant of representation, you can write immediately to each institution holding the assets (for example banks or building societies) enclosing a copy and asking for the funds to be released to you.

It is usual to set up a new bank account for the purposes of settling the estate; banks can advise you on how to set up an executor's account. Cheques received from financial institutions, and any money raised from the sale of assets, can then be paid into this account, making it easier to produce the estate accounts and making sure the money belonging to the estate is kept separate from your own money.

You will need to keep a clear record of any expenses resulting from your role as personal representative. This could be things like postage, travel costs, copying costs, fees etc. You should keep receipts for all your expenses as these can be claimed back from the estate.

Benefits

If the deceased was in receipt of state benefits you should contact the relevant office as soon as possible. This is because there may be arrears owed to the estate or an overpayment that needs to be paid back. You, or whoever registered the death, would have been given a certificate of registration of death (form BD8) which you need to use to provide information to the Jobcentre Plus, or the Pension Service, depending on what benefits they were receiving.

Income tax

It could be that there will be an income tax rebate due to the estate or that a final tax bill will have to be paid. You should inform the relevant tax office as soon as possible about the death. The relevant office will either be that nearest the deceased's home address, or place of business if they were self-employed, or their employer's tax office if they were working or drawing an occupational pension. Details of how to find a local tax office are in chapter 9. The HMRC Deceased Estates helpline can give advice on income tax issues relating to estates on *0131 777 4030*.

Paying any debts

All debts and money owing must be paid before the estate can be distributed to the beneficiaries.

This would include any mortgage, unless the will stated that property was to be passed on subject to the existing mortgage and the mortgage company agrees to the beneficiary taking this on. It would also include any unpaid household bills, legal costs if you have used a solicitor or outstanding funeral costs. If bills such as council tax have been paid in advance, there could be money to be claimed back for the estate.

If it looks like there isn't enough money to pay all the debts, you may need to take legal advice. There is a priority order in which debts must be paid. If you don't pay them in the right order and one of the priority debts is unpaid, you, as the personal representative, could be personally liable to pay it from your own money.

Similarly, if you go ahead and distribute the estate and later discover an unpaid debt which you weren't aware of, you could be personally liable to pay it. You can protect yourself from liability by advertising for any creditors. If you place an advert in the *London Gazette* and in a local paper for the area where the deceased last lived, and then wait two months before distributing the estate, you should not be liable if a previously unknown creditor later comes forward. It may seem strange to advertise in the *London Gazette* (especially if the person who died didn't live in London) but this is traditionally where these adverts have been placed and is the accepted way of protecting yourself from unknown creditors.

Distribute the estate

It is only once you are confident that you have collected in all the assets, paid all the debts and paid the final IHT bill, if any, that you can go ahead and distribute money, possessions and property to the beneficiaries, as set out in the will or under the intestacy rules.

If the deceased owned their own home, it may be necessary to sell this, in order to pay off the mortgage or to be able to pay out legacies to beneficiaries unless an alternative agreement can be reached between the beneficiaries. If the home is to be transferred to a beneficiary, or the deceased's share automatically passes to another joint owner, you will need to register this with the Land Registry. You can obtain guidance on how to do this from the Land Registry or you might want to get help from a solicitor.

If any of the beneficiaries are under age 18, the property or money should be held on trust for them (see page 21). You may need to seek advice on this.

If the estate includes shares, and it is necessary to sell these, you will need to go through a stockbroker. If the will says the shares are to be transferred directly to a beneficiary, this can be done by completing a 'stock transfer' form (available from law stationers, banks or building societies, or from the registrar of the company in which the shares are held) and returning this to the registrar of the company the shares are held with who can update their records and issue new share certificates in the name of the beneficiary.

When you distribute the legacies, ask beneficiaries to sign receipts to confir have received. There is no standard fo but the receipts should state exactly w received what and when, in case any d arises in the future.

It is a good idea to keep a clear list of everything in the estate and how it is distributed. Your notes should show all the capital and income which made up the estate; if everything has gone to plan, this should match up with your list showing what has been distributed.

You have a duty to make all reasonable efforts to find a beneficiary or, if there is no will, to find anyone who is entitled to a share under the intestacy rules. If you can't find a particular beneficiary, you should advertise for anyone who thinks they have a claim against the estate to come forward. There are probate genealogy companies which specialise in searching for missing beneficiaries. You can also take out insurance to cover the risk that someone unknown to you will come forward to claim their share when you have already given it to someone else.

Claims against the estate

Someone who was dependent on the deceased who feels they have not been provided for fairly in the will or under the intestacy rules can make a claim on the estate. They have six months from the grant of representation within which to make a claim. This could be a spouse, civil partner, or former spouse or civil partner, a child of the deceased, a partner who lived with them for at two years before their death or someone else who was financially dependent on them. They can claim if they have not been left 'reasonable financial provision'. This will be for the court to decide. If this situation arises, you should seek legal advice before you distribute anything.

Summary

Being a personal representative can involve a lot of work and responsibility, depending on the nature of the estate, and it can take a long time before everything is finalised. But if you keep in mind the basic tasks involved – to collect in the estate, pay any money owing and distribute what is left – it needn't be such a daunting prospect, especially as you have the option of seeking professional advice when you need it. Being able to choose the most appropriate person for the role is a good reason for making your own will.

9
More help

Age Concern England
1268 London Road, London
SW16 4ER
Tel: 0800 0099 66 information
line
www.ageconcern.org.uk
*ACE offers help, advice and
support to older people, their
carers and relatives.
Information and factsheets
can be ordered from the
information line or
downloaded direct from the
website.*

Age Concern Cymru
Ty John Pathy, Unit 13 and
14 Neptune Court,
Vanguard Way, Cardiff
CF24 5PJ
Tel: 029 2043 1555
www.accymru.org.uk

Action on Elder Abuse
Astral House, 1268 London
Road, Norbury, London
SW16 4ER
Tel: 0808 808 8141
www.elderabuse.org.uk
*A confidential helpline
providing information and
advice for anyone concerned
about the abuse of older
people.*

AdviceNow
www.advicenow.org.uk
*An independent not-for-profit
website providing free legal
information.*

Alzheimer's Society
Dementia Helpline, Devon
House, 58 St Katharine's
Way, London E1W 1JX
Tel: 0845 300 0336
www.alzheimers.org.uk
*For information and advice
on dementia, including lasting
powers of attorney and
advance decisions.*

Bereavement Advice Centre
Ryon Hill House, Ryon Hill
Park, Warwick Road,
Stratford upon Avon
CV37 0UX
Tel: 0800 634 9494
*A not-for-profit organisation
giving practical information
and advice on what to do
after someone has died.*

The Bereavement Register
Freepost SEA8240,
Sevenoaks TN13 1XR
Tel: 0870 600 7222
www.the-bereavement-
register.org.uk

A service aimed at preventing direct mail being sent to deceased people.

Bona Vacantia Division,
Treasury Solicitor's Office (BV), One Kemble Street, London WC2B 4TS.
www.bonavacantia.gov.uk
Deals with estates where the person has died intestate and there are no known family members.

Charities Aid Foundation
25 Kings Hill Avenue, Kings Hill, West Malling, Kent ME19 4TA
Tel: 01732 520355
www.cafonline.org
Can give advice on leaving a legacy to a charity.

CIFAS
PO Box 1141, Bradford BD1 5UR
Tel: 0870 010 2091
www.cifas.org.uk
Can help protect against fraudulent use of a deceased person's identity.

Citizens Advice Bureau
For details of your local CAB go to www.citizensadvice. org.uk *or look in your local phone book. Online information is available at* www.adviceguide.org.uk.

Community Legal Advice
Tel: 0845 345 4 345
www.communitylegaladvice. org.uk
A free legal advice service for people entitled to Legal Aid. Call the helpline or go to the website to find out if you are eligible. Free information is available on the website.

Cruse Bereavement Care
PO Box 800, Richmond, Surrey TW9 1RG
Tel: 0844 477 9400
www.crusebereavementcare. org.uk
A counselling and advice service for bereaved people offering practical support.

Financial Ombudsman Service
South Quay Plaza, 183 Marsh Walk, London E14 9SR
Tel: 020 7964 1000
www.financial-ombudsman. org.uk
The official independent expert in settling complaints between consumers and businesses providing financial services.

Financial Services Authority
25 The North Colonnade, Canary Wharf, London E14 5HS
Tel: 0845 606 1234
www.fsa.gov.uk
An independent body regulating the financial

services industry in the UK.
The FSA can confirm whether
a financial adviser is
authorised.

Free Wills Month
Tel: 0845 020 4309
www.freewillsmonth.org.uk
*A scheme which encourages
people aged 55 and over to
have their will written free of
charge by a local solicitor.
The hope is that users of the
scheme will leave a gift in
their will to one or more
of the charities that fund the
scheme, although there is no
obligation to do so.*

General Register Office
PO Box 2, Southport,
Merseyside PR8 2JD
Tel: 0845 603 7788
(enquiries about applying for
death certificates)
Tel: 0151 471 4805
(enquiries about death
registration procedures)
www.gro.gov.uk
*The GRO registers and
supplies official information on
births, marriages and deaths
and where to find local
registery officies.*

Help the Aged
207-221 Pentonville Road,
London N1 9UZ
Tel: 0808 800 6565
(Seniorline)
www.helptheagod.org.uk
For a wide range of

information and advice for
older people.

**HM Revenue & Customs
(HMRC)**
Tel: 0131 777 4030
(Deceased estates helpline
for informatin on income tax
and capital gains tax)
Tel: 0845 302 0900 (Probate
and inheritance tax helpline)
www.hmrc.gov.uk
*For details of local tax offices
see the local phone book or
go to the website.*

**Institute of Chartered
Accountants in England
and Wales**
www.icaewfirms.co.uk
*To search online for details of
accountants specialising in
estate and inheritance tax
issues.*

**Institute of Professional
Will Writers**
Trinity Point, New Road,
Halesowen, West Midlands
B63 3HY
Tel: 08456 442042
www.ipw.org.uk
*Voluntary regulatory body of
will writers*

Land Registry
www.landregistry.gov.uk
*For details of your local land
registry office, see your local
phone book*

Law Society *(office in London)*
The Law Society's Hall,
113 Chancery Lane, London
WC2A 1PL
Tel: 020 7242 1222
www.lawsociety.org.uk
Law Society *(office in Wales)*
Capital Tower, Greyfriars
Road, Cardiff CF10 3AG
Tel: 29 2064 5254
To find a solicitor

Legal Complaints Service
Victoria Court, 8 Dormer
Place, Leamington Spa,
Warwickshire CV32 5AE
Tel: 0845 608 6565
www.legalcomplaints.org.uk

Lesbian and Gay Bereavement Project
Counselling Department,
Lighthouse West London,
111-117 Lancaster Road,
London W11 1QT
Tel: 020 7403 5969 (Helpline)
The helpline offers a listening ear to lesbians and gay men who have been bereaved or are preparing for bereavement as well as to family and friends, colleagues and carers.

Mailing Preference Service
DMA House, 70 Margaret
Street, London W1W 8SS
Tel: 0845 703 4599
www.mpsonline.org.uk/mpsr/
A service that can prevent direct mail being sent to deceased people.

National Association of Funeral Directors
618 Warwick Road, Solihull,
West Midlands B91 1AA
Tel: 0845 230 1343
www.nafd.org.uk
Voluntary regulatory body

Natural Death Centre
Blackstock Mews,
Blackstock Road, London
N4 2BT
Tel: 0871 288 2098
www.naturaldeath.org.uk
For information on different types of funeral.

Office of the Public Guardian
Archway Tower, 2 Junction
Road, London N19 5SZ
Tel: 0845 330 2900
www.publicguardian.gov.uk
For information and advice on mental capacity issues including lasting powers of attorney and the court of protection.

The Patients Association
PO Box 935, Harrow,
Middlesex HA1 3JY
Tel: 0845 608 4455 (Helpline)
Produces information materials, including on living wills.

The Principal Registry
Safe Custody Clerk, Record
Keeper's Department, First
Avenue House, 42–49 High
Holborn, London WC1V 6NP

For storing your will at the Principal Registry (the principal probate registry in London) or searching to see if someone else's will has been deposited there.

Probate Registries
Tel: 0845 30 20 900 (Probate and Inheritance tax helpline)
www.hmcourts-service.gov.uk
For contact details of local probate registries, call the Probate and Inheritance tax helpline.

Society of Trust and Estate Practitioners (STEP)
Artillery House (South), 11-19 Artillery Row, London SW1P 1RT
www.step.org
To find a solicitor or accountant specialising in estate planning.

The Society of Will Writers & Estate Planning Practitioners
Eagle House, Exchange Road, Lincoln LN6 3JZ
Tel: 01522 687888
www.willwriters.com
Voluntary regulatory body

Solicitors for the Elderly
Room 17, Conbar House, Mead Lane, Hertford SG13 7AP
Tel: 0870 067 0282
www.solicitorsfortheelderly.com

Organisation of solicitors, barristers and legal executives committed to providing and promoting independent legal advice for older people, their families and carers.

Solicitors' Regulation Authority
Ipsley Court, Berrington Close, Redditch B98 0TD
Tel: 0870 606 2555
www.sra.org.uk
For details of solicitors in England and Wales.

Unbiased.co.uk
www.unbiased.co.uk
To search online for local independent financial advisers.

Unclaimed Assets Register
PO Box 9501, Nottingham NG80 1WD
Tel: 0870 241 1713
This is a service to help people trace forgotten or lost assets such as pensions or insurance policies.

Will Aid
Roundham House, Oxen Road, Crewkerne, Somerset TA18 7HN
Tel: 0300 0300 013
A scheme run every November under which a local solicitor will draw up your will for free in return for a suggested donation to a group of charities.

Information for people in Scotland

Age Concern Scotland
Causewayside House,
160 Causewayside,
Edinburgh
EH9 1PR
Tel: 0845 125 9732 (Scottish Helpline for Older People)
www.ageconcernscotland.org.uk

Citizens Advice Bureau
www.adviceguide.org.uk/scotland
The online CAB information and advice service. To find your local CAB go to www.cas.org.uk, or call 0131 550 1000 (no advice can be given on this number).

General Register Office for Scotland
Ladywell House, Ladywell Road, Edinburgh EH12 7TH
Tel: 0131 334 0380
www.gro-scotland.gov.uk
The website includes information on how to register a death in Scotland.

The Law Society of Scotland
26 Drumsheugh Gardens,
Edinburgh EH3 7YR
Tel: 0131 226 7411
www.lawscot.org.uk
For details of solicitors in Scotland.

Office of the Public Guardian (Scotland)
Hadrian House, Callendar Business Park, Callendar Road, Falkirk FK1 1XR
Tel: 01324 678300
www.publicguardian-scotland.gov.uk
For information and advice on decision making for people who may lack mental capacity.

The Scottish Government
Civil and International Justice Directorate
Area 2W, St Andrew's House, Regent Road, Edinburgh
EH1 3DG
Tel. 0131 244 2193
www.scotland.gov.uk
You can obtain the booklet 'What to do after a death in Scotland' from this address and website. You can also obtain the booklet 'It's your decision' which covers the law on mental capacity in Scotland.

Will Relief Scotland
Queens Building, George Street, Oban PA34 5RZ
Tel: 01631 562308
A scheme run in Scotland every May under which a solicitor will draw up your will for free in return for a suggested donation to a group of overseas aid charities.

Information for people in Northern Ireland

Age Concern Northern Ireland
3 Lower Crescent, Belfast
BT7 1NR
Tel: 028 9032 5055
www.ageconcernni.org

Citizens Advice
www.adviceguide.org.uk/
nireland
*The online CAB information
and advice service. To find
your local CAB go to
www.citizensadvice.co.uk, or
call 028 9023 1120 (no advice
can be given on this number).*

General Register Office (Northern Ireland)
Oxford House, 49/55
Chichester Street, Belfast
BT1 4HL
Tel: 028 90 252000
www.groni.gov.uk
*For information on registering
a death.*

The Law Society of Northern Ireland
40 Linenhall Street, Belfast
BT2 8BA
Tel: 028 9023 1614
www.lawsoc-ni.org
*For details of solicitors in
Northern Ireland*

10
Glossary

Administrator Someone appointed to deal with an estate if there are no executors, either because the deceased did not leave a will or because the named executors cannot or do not wish to act. Also known as a personal representative.

Advance decision A decision to refuse a certain type of medical treatment in the future if the person making it cannot make the decision themselves at the relevant time. Advance decisions are often called living wills.

Advance statement Any statement, other than a decision to refuse medical treatment, that indicates a person's wishes and preferences for their care or treatment if they become unable to make those decisions for themselves.

Attorney A person given the authority to make decisions and act on behalf of someone else under a lasting power of attorney.

Beneficiary A person, organisation or charity who receives something in a will or under the intestacy rules.

Bequest A gift made in a will (also called a legacy).

Certificate provider Someone (either a suitable professional or someone who has known the person making an LPA for at least two years) who signs a lasting power of attorney to confirm that the person creating it understands the purpose and effect of the document and has not been put under undue pressure to make it.

Codicil A document adding to, or amending, an existing will.

Contingent legacy A gift made in a will which will only take effect in particular circumstances if something changes after the will is made for example, if a beneficiary dies before the will writer.

Court of Protection The Court of Protection has the power to make decisions relating to people who may lack capacity to make their own decisions.

Deputy Someone appointed by the Court of Protection to make decisions on behalf of someone who may lack mental capacity.

Discretionary trust A type of trust often set up under a will, giving the trustees flexibility over how the assets are dealt with. Changes to the rules allowing the transfer of the IHT nil-rate band mean discretionary trusts are no longer needed in many situations.

Estate The possessions property, money and investments owned by someone at the time of their death.

Executor Someone named in a will as a person who is to deal with the estate. Also known as a personal representative.

Funeral plan A commercial scheme to allow people to pay in advance for their own funeral, at a fixed price, either in instalments or a lump sum.

Grant of representation The document that proves that a personal representative has authority to deal with the estate of someone who has died. This can be either a grant of probate (if it is for an executor) or letters of administration (if it is for an administrator).

Inheritance tax (IHT) A tax which is paid out of someone's estate if their taxable estate is worth more than the current IHT threshold. It is calculated on the value of an estate after a person's death and on gifts during their lifetime in some circumstances.

Inheritance tax (IHT) threshold The amount of money above which IHT is payable. If the value of a taxable estate is below the threshold, no IHT is payable. The threshold amount is set by the Government each year.

Intestate Someone dies intestate if they have died without making a valid will.

Intestacy rules The rules that apply if someone has died without making a valid will, to determine who will inherit their estate and how it will be divided.

Joint tenants Joint tenancy is one of two ways of owning property jointly with someone else. If property is owned as joint tenants, on the death of one of the owners, their share will pass automatically to the surviving joint owner(s). It cannot be left to someone else in a will. See 'tenancy in common'

Lasting power of attorney (LPA) A document by which someone gives one or more people (attorneys) authority to make decisions on their behalf if they lack mental capacity to make those decisions themselves. There are different types of LPA to cover either decisions about the donor's property and financial affairs or their health and welfare.

Legacy A gift made in a will (also called a bequest).

Letters of administration The document granted to an administrator proving they have authority to deal with the estate, where there is no will or no executors able or willing to act. Also known as a grant of representation.

Life interest Someone with a life interest in an asset, such as money or property, can enjoy the benefit of that asset during their lifetime but cannot dispose of it. On the death of the person with the life interest the asset passes to someone else.

Living will A term sometimes used to refer to either advance decisions, or advance statements.

Mental capacity Having mental capacity means being able to make a decision for yourself about a particular matter. To be able to make the decision, you must be able to understand and retain the information relevant to the decision, understand the implications and be able to communicate the decision.

Nil-rate band The proportion of an estate which is below the IHT threshold, on which no IHT is payable.

Office of the Public Guardian The Public Guardian keeps a register of lasting powers of attorney, and enduring powers of attorney, and is responsible for dealing with concerns about how attorneys and deputies are carrying out their duties.

Partial intestacy If a will does not specify what is to happen to the remainder of an estate, or if the beneficiary of the remainder has died, there will be a partial intestacy. The intestacy rules will apply to determine who inherits the remainder.

Pecuniary legacy A gift made in a will of a specific amount of money.

Personal representative The person with authority to deal with an estate of someone who has died. This can either be an executor or an administrator.

Potentially exempt transfer A gift to an individual on which IHT can become payable if the transferor dies within seven years of making the gift.

Probate The document granted to an executor, proving that they have authority to deal with the estate.

Probate registry A local office responsible for issuing and advising on grants of representation.

Register office A local office responsible for the registration of births, marriages and deaths. Local register offices in England and Wales are overseen by the General Register Office.

Registrar The officer responsible for the registration of births, marriages and deaths.

Remainder What remains of an estate after all debts and specific or pecuniary legacies have been paid.

Residuary beneficiary The person, charity or organisation named to inherit the remainder of your estate.

Residuary legacy A gift of the remainder of an estate after all other gifts have been made. The remainder can also be called the residue of your estate.

Specific legacy A gift made in a will of a particular item or piece of property.

Taxable estate The possessions, property, money and investments owned by someone at the time of their death which may be taxed under the inheritance tax rules

Tenants in common One of two ways of owning property jointly with someone else. If property is owned as tenants in common, on the death of one of the owners their share will pass to their estate (not to the other owner as with a joint tenancy). Whoever inherits this share will then own the property jointly in common with the other original owner(s).

Trust A way of holding assets for the benefit of someone else, without that person having ownership of them. For example, money can be held by trustees for a child and the money can be invested and/or spent for the child's benefit before they are entitled to inherit ownership of it themselves at age 18.

Will writer Someone offering a commercial will drafting service who is not a solicitor.

Index

About Age Concern

Age Concern is the UK's largest organisation working for and with older people to enable them to make more of life. We are a federation of over 400 independent charities who share the same name, values and standards and believe that later life should be fulfilling, enjoyable and productive.

Age Concern England
1268 London Road
London SW16 4ER
SW16 4ER
Tel: 020 8765 7200
www.ageconcern.org.uk

Age Concern Cymru
Ty John Pathy
Units 13 and 14 Neptune Court
Vanguard Way, Cardiff CF24 5PJ
Tel: 029 2043 1555
www.accymru.org.uk

Age Concern Scotland
Causewayside House
160 Causewayside
Edinburgh EH9 1PP
Tel: 0845 833 0200
www.ageconcernscotland.org.uk

Age Concern Northern Ireland
3 Lower Crescent
Belfast BT7 1NR
Tel: 028 9024 5729
www.ageconcernni.org

Age Concern Books

Age Concern publishes a wide range of bestselling books that help thousands of people each year. They provide practical, trusted advice on subjects ranging from pensions and planning for retirement, to using a computer and surfing the internet. Whether you are caring for someone with a health problem or want to know more about your rights to healthcare, we have something for everyone.

Ordering is easy To order any of our books or request our free catalogue simply choose one of the following options:

☎ **Call us on 0870 44 22 120**

🖱 **Visit our website at www.ageconcern.org.uk/bookshop**

 Email us at sales@ageconcernbooks.co.uk

You can also buy our books from all good bookshops.